THE ART OF GETTING IT DONE

The Art of Getting It Done

Secrets of Overachievers and How Anyone Can Be One

DR. CHRISTINE TOPJIAN

Christine Topjian Publishing

Contents

Publishing Information — vii
Other Books By The Author — ix
Dedications — xi

INTRODUCTION

1	Actually Doing It	4
2	Cutting The Chatter	6
3	Two Traits That Stand Out	16
4	God At The Center	22
5	Focus In Real, Everyday Terms	28
6	Journaling With The Holy Spirit	46
7	Visualize With The Help Of The Holy Spirit	54
8	Strategic, Inspired, Consistent Action	60
9	Documenting	65
10	Eliminate Hurtful, Harmful, Detrimental Thoughts As Much As Possible	71
11	The Inconvenient	79
12	Learning Something New	90
13	BIG Goals	97

14	Helpful Angels	104
15	Managing Disappointment	108
16	Managing Stress & The Inconvenient - The Drive To Succeed	115
17	Taking The Time, Doing It Right	126
18	Self-Assuredness	130
19	Many Things	133
20	Discover What And/Or Who Inspires You	137
21	Glory To God	141
22	Going Back	143

IMAGES

Notes   161
Thanks   165

Publishing Information

Published by Christine Topjian Publishing
(An Imprint of Authors Get Published)
AuthorsGetPublished.com

Toronto, ON

Copyright © 2022 by Dr. Christine Topjian

All rights reserved. No part of this publication may be reproduced, distributed, or transmitted in any form or by any means, including photocopying, recording, or other electronic or mechanical methods, without the prior written permission of the publisher, except in the case of brief quotations embodied in critical reviews and certain other noncommercial uses permitted by copyright law.

Other Books By The Author

"Check out the many books by Award-winning Author, Dr. Christine Topjian at DrChristineTopjian.com"

Other books by Dr. Christine Topjian (and counting):

Jesus Loves You

Love & Kindness

Give it to God

Hannah Can Read

It's in Transit

How to Be Led by the Holy Spirit

Are You Ready for God's Best for Your Life?

The Chrissie Series: Chrissie Meditates & Visualizes

The Chrissie Series: Chrissie Goes Places

The Chrissie Series: Chrissie Prays

The Chrissie Series: Chrissie Speaks Nicely

The Power of the Give

God & Prosperity

Manifest It!

Manifest It ... Now!

Etes-vous prêts pour le meilleur de Dieu?

THE MONEY MANUAL

The Art of Getting It Done

Dedications

Dedications

This book is dedicated to my loving parents, Dr. Garo and Mrs. Vivian Topjian.

Thank you both for everything you did and you continue to do!

Introduction

Overachievers.

They are leaders and they are present in every industry.

They are people who lead busy lives but still make time to get everything done. While others are sleeping, they are strategically working. While others may be unsure of themselves, they are assuredly getting it done. Finished. Complete. On to the next.

Overachievers are people who complete things and do so to the best of their abilities. They set a tone and a benchmark that others often want to emulate. They set a way that others often want to discover. They are people who don't allow circumstances to get in their way. These are no excuses kind of people.

You too can be one of these people, if you are not already.

Who Are They?

They are people who come from all walks of life, have been through a great variety of things and consistently work their hardest despite any challenges they face. They are people who work with an exemplary diligence because they understand that that is what is necessary. Is there a specific profile for this type of person? No, they are just the ones who work the most strategic and with resolve.

It's the young person who may come from a dysfunctional home and goes to the library to study for hours upon hours because they know that this education and law degree are what they are going to need to build themselves a better life.

It's the older person who doesn't accept being inactive but works hard at their job or at understanding how something works and makes it their priority to remain abreast of new trends and forecasts.

It's the middle aged person who got beat out by another for the promotion but never mind...he or she is going to work strategically on how to do so much better than even that job they were gunning for.

It's the single parent who juggles their full time work and also juggles their children, doing their very best to be there for their family and to help their families in any way they can.

It's the person who was never taught how to do what they know they need to but they gathered the resources they needed and figured out how. They did not stop until they finished it.

Overachievers are focused, determined, strategic, no-nonsense, and they are good at cutting the chatter.

> One of the qualities that sets this book apart from other books about overachieving is that this one includes God in the equation. Why? Because we were never meant to get it all done on our own. Far from it. We were and are always meant to take on great endeavors in tandem with Him and with His help and careful guidance.

If you do not yet identify with being an overachiever or a person who gets things done, then this book will help you to get to that level. This book will help you get to the frame of mind that is needed to accomplish all that you have been called to do.

Another wonderful thing about being an overachiever is how you positively influence others around you. People get influenced and inspired by those around them all the time. When you do wonderful things and you work hard and build a wonderful life for yourself, you inevitably inspire others to do the same for themselves. It's a win-win situation.

Happy reading and happy doing!

Chapter 1

Actually Doing It

A book about overachievers needs to begin (I believe) with one of the most important and basic concepts: **actually doing it**. This means actually doing the planning, the strategizing, the hard work.

Many people can pick up a book like this and can find it interesting to read (great if you do), but taking it a step beyond that is actually doing the work that is required so that you can actually achieve all that you need to. You see, being an overachiever and one who gets things done actually means that it will require a massive amount of all of the following: faith, planning, action, patience, perseverance, God's help and more.

But I want to be clear here: you have to actually do the work.

Success does not ultimately come from just wishing to be successful. It comes from the many steps that are required and then actually doing the work. Not allowing oneself to get distracted but to actually get it all done. Dealing with giving up alternate ways (maybe more fun ways) to spend your time but knowing that sacrifice is absolutely necessary on the road to success. Not allowing oneself to be distracted by naysayers who are working to bring you down and to cause yourself to doubt what you are doing but working hard in the face of all of that.

An example comes to mind: I was spending time with someone who had indicated that she really wanted to get a book of poetry written and published. She had talked about this many times before and I was supportive of this endeavor and when she told me about the premise for the poems, I got excited about her book. I reminded her that she had talked about this before and about how much doing this meant to her, so I encouraged her to set down and to start writing and compiling. You see, she had already written many of the poems over the years so it was now just a matter of putting it all together nicely and then I would have helped her with the publishing side of things. She said that she would start writing and compiling that very night. When I checked in later in the evening, she had unfortunately not begun but indicated that she would first thing the next day. That didn't happen either. Day after day I would check in with her but she still had not found time to get started.

Readers, we all have busy lives and I respect that. Bear in mind that when you say that you want to accomplish something but you don't take the first step or you indefinitely procrastinate the first step, that you are not on the right path to the successful completion of what you say is important to you.

Hence, the first lesson: actually working on it.

Chapter 2

Cutting The Chatter

In order to work in a focused and strategic manner, we sometimes have to cut out the chatter.

Why?

Because sometimes the chatter (the conversation, the distractions, the naysayers) is extra and we don't need it. You don't need to know what 100 people think about something or their experiences with it before you get started. You need to know the facts about it and then you need to pray over it for the Holy Spirit to show us our way with it. Getting caught up in chatter is not usually helpful because people often have many opinions about things and they often derail us. Instead, we have to listen to the Holy Spirit, be focused in our work and on our goals, and actually do what we are being guided to do - that is not going to happen when you are spending your time listening to everyone around you.

To provide an example: a friend of mine who wanted to start her own business was on social media. On social media, she joined a group of like-minded business people who were sort of in the same "boat" as her - starting a business and she began to read about their thoughts, excitements, worries, hesitations and more. You may think this is helpful but it wasn't. She spent hours per day reading through the comments, and frankly, psyching herself out. She began to worry and to have hesitations about what she was going and began to talk herself out of it.

The important question is: what is the Holy Spirit telling you to do about it? Is the idea from God? If it is, then you will receive clear instructions about how to move forward in an intelligent and strategic way because that's Who the Holy Spirit is - a strategic, loving and patient Counselor who will show you the best way.

I knew I was being called to write books. Chapter books with lots of good teaching in them and I was being guided to do it through my own publishing house because that meant I had the most control over the books, distribution, pricing and much more. But at the time, I felt unable to write chapter books. I had only written short books with illustrations until that point and didn't feel I could write a longer chapter book. So I prayed about it and asked the Holy Spirit how I could do this because this was something that was important to me. At the time, I was looking to see the experiences of other writers too because I thought that would help me (and my process) a lot. It didn't. I heard (well, read) about the experiences of others on social media and all it did was discourage me and distract me from doing what I needed to do - write!

So, upon the guidance and instructions from the Holy Spirit, I turned off social media. I logged off and began thinking and praying over it. The guidance was clear: the Holy Spirit gave me several ways in which I could focus on what I needed to do and some strategies for staying focused. I realized that some very simple practices could, would and did make a big difference: for example, I realized that keeping my manuscript open on my laptop made a big difference. In other words, I would keep that tab open on my laptop for as long as I needed to, until I finished writing the entire manuscript AND reviewed it AND checked it all over for grammar, typos, editing, meaning, etc. I kept the document open so that I wouldn't forget about it and it would remind me every single time I opened my laptop to do anything that the manuscript was still there, not finished yet and reminded me constantly that I needed to get that book written because it was meaningful and important. This worked really well because it was a consistent (sometimes slightly annoying reminder) to get the work done.

Being on social media for extended periods of time was nice to chat with some people but was never the tool that gave me the consistent kick in the pants to strive for better.

I began to realize through my prayers that many authors and people in general talk about how it should take months or even years to write their book. The Holy Spirit interjected that thought and reminded me that that was simply not the needed reality. It doesn't need to take you that long if you are focused, work diligently and yes, sacrifice other things in order to get the book done. So I did that. I sat down and wrote and wrote and wrote and re-read and corrected and wrote and wrote and wrote. I also had a separate tab open where I would journal and ask the Holy Spirit for help and for advice and for renewed ideas and a renewed spirit to keep on going and to add in the information and the ideas that would be needed. I began to see how prayer, focus and discipline were the driving forces behind accomplishing what needed to be accomplished and how God would guide you to His best in order to get the right things done.

I saw that I became more focused and accomplished and that when I cut out the clutter and the chatter, I became a more productive writer and publisher, able to put out much more quality pieces within a shorter amount of time.

I actually began to find new joy in my work and began to really see myself as a writer of a variety of books in different lengths, flavors and genres, each being an important part of my writing repertoire.

I tell you this so that you too can find your stride. You can find out through the Holy Spirit what is your way.

Here are some more examples to help you find your way, to motivate you and to help you see that many others are in the same boat:

Julia's Exercise

When she knew she needed to lose weight and be determined about it, Julia closed the door to her home exercise room, put a piece of fabric on the treadmill's monitor, wore her support-filled running shoes and got to work. She ran and did cardio until her body felt like it might collapse. She was focused, determined, and didn't ask 15 friends before getting started. She prayed about it and then, just did it. Was it easy for Julia? No, she had to build up to being able to do 4 minutes of cardio, then 6, then 8 and so on. She didn't start by becoming a world-famous runner but she worked hard at it and yes, she had to give up other fun things she would have liked to do instead in order to achieve her goals of being more fit, lean and healthier.

You can too.

Mark's Masters Degree

When he knew he needed to complete his Masters and he began to be determined about it, Mark closed the door to his study room, turned off his phone, checked in with his family to let them know not to disturb him and got to work. He opened those books and began to pour over the exercises he had to do, he ate his meals at his desk with the only breaks being to do a short workout or to read to his kids, and he only opened the door to his study room when he was completely finished with the section he felt guided that he had to complete for that day. He did this day after day, week after week, month after month. He was focused, determined, and didn't ask 15 friends before getting started. He prayed about it and just did it.

You can too.

Lorenzo's Real Estate Firm

When Lorenzo knew that he needed to complete his real estate license in order to begin conducting real estate transactions in his home town of Colorado, he knew it was going to take money, time and hard work. He had a family to support and his wife was not working as she was taking care of the kids but he had gotten laid off at his construction job and believed (with much prayer) that this was the right path for him. He began to work at it. He used some of the money he had saved, applied for some scholarships, bought used books and had the internet connection to get done what he needed to get done. He worked hard each day, completing section after section, passing the little quizzes along the way, gave up spending time with his family and his friends, even missing a friend's birthday because one of his exams fell on the exact same day. He worked hard at it and he tried his best never to complain. When he discovered that he had not passed one of his exams that he had studied very hard for, he decided it may be helpful to join a study group. He benefited from the additional help and from the study resources the group was using and he passed that difficult exam with flying colors. He worked on visualizing the final goal and how he would feel having accomplished his goal of having his license and being able to practice real estate within his own firm. He visualized how this may help his children one day as they might also like to get involved in the field and he prayed regularly for God to help him see things with this endeavor the way he needed to see them. He was focused, determined, and didn't ask 15 friends before getting started. He prayed about it and just did it.

You can too.

Betty's Pregnancy Journey

When Betty knew that she and her husband wanted to get pregnant with their second and began to be determined about it, Betty began to be very focused. She made sure that they found a babysitter for their daughter, that they were able to have private time for each other, she began taking her supplements and reading books on rearing a second child and she made regular appointments to see her doctor for follow-ups. She poured over those pregnancy books and went to the store to look for a second crib, blankets and tons of new baby clothes for their second baby. She also dedicated herself to eating well, taking any and all vitamins and ensuring that she was doing everything she needed to do to get pregnant for the second time. She prioritized special alone time with her husband even when he was busy at work and didn't have a lot of time, they agreed as a couple that this would be part of their focus. Betty was focused, determined, and didn't ask 15 friends before getting started. She prayed about it and just did it.

You can too.

Jenny's Financial Goals

When Jenny knew that she wanted a certain amount of money and to retire early, she knew that she would need great resolve to accomplish this. Her family didn't have much money and she never grew up with much, and she knew that the examples around her were not great in terms of accomplishments. She knew that she would need to get a new money framework and that she would need a great amount of God's blessings to get this accomplished. Jenny's family growing up had negative views about money and so she was never taught that she could have anything more than a paycheck to paycheck living but she knew she wanted much more for herself than that. So, she began to focus and got to work praying. She began listening carefully to what the Holy Spirit was saying to her and so she began doing all of the following: 1) never wasting her money on unnecessary frills 2) she began tithing to organizations the Holy Spirit was leading her to support 3) she began clipping coupons and making sure she never spent more than she had to on groceries, clothes and needed essentials 4) she got a part time job and began making extra money 5) she read books and listened to audio podcasts about Christian billionaires

Jenny was extremely diligent in her efforts and was so for years. She turned around one day and realized that due to her efforts, and obedience, she had amassed enough for a very healthy down payment on a lovely home. She was so pleased with herself and knew that she was making great strides because nobody in her family line had ever owned a home. She prayed about it and did it as she was led.

You can too.

Robert's Paralympic Dreams

Robert is a brilliant young man who loves to ski. He had been skiing since he was a young boy living in Canada, when his mother used to take him and his brother Raphael to the local ski park so that they could learn to ski. Robert really took to skiing and loved being on the slopes. He loved it so much that he entered a competition and won first place. Robert would spend hours and hours going down the slopes, enjoying the rush of fresh, crisp cool air as it hit his face in a refreshing way and he loved being on his skis. He entered more competitions and won the top 3 spots in each competition. When he turned 10, Robert was in a very bad vehicle collision that left him unable to walk. His doctors told him and his family that he would likely never walk again and his family considered his skiing dreams to be a thing of the past. Not Robert. Robert knew that with hard work, time, healing and rehabilitation, he would be able to compete in skiing competitions again. After two years of healing and rehabilitation, Robert signed up for a skiing competition for people who were physically disabled. His family thought it was too soon but Robert found himself a coach who would show him how to use the limbs and the limb functions he still had and use them to his advantage. With months of focused work and continued rehab, Robert got back some use of his legs and was able to step into skis again. It was extraordinarily painful to do so but he managed to get back into those skis and he was able to begin winning competitions for those with physical disabilities. Robert's resolve, focus, determination and persistence were and are awe-inspiring. He was focused, determined, and didn't ask 15 friends before getting started. He prayed over it, felt led by the Spirit and then, he did it.

You can too.

The concept is the same whatever your name is, whoever you are and whatever your history is and whatever your background is (background includes family history, education, ethnic background, and more). It is really important for you to get into the right frame of mind and to stay the course, following how the Holy Spirit prompts you each step of the way. You will be really happy you did because when you are being guided and you are obedient in that guidance, you will see things work in your favor. It may take some time and you will need to be patient, but it will happen in God's timing and in His way.

Your Attitude During The Wait

Another really important point to make here is that your attitude while you are working on something really matters. If you are going through your day grumbling, complaining, upset and dissatisfied, you are not waiting in the right way. It is important to wait with gratitude and positive expectancy. It is important to have such faith that you give thanks to God for providing it before you can actually see it in front of you. This does make the blessing appear more quickly. Here are the passages in Scripture that indicate this

"The Lord is good to those who wait for him, to the soul who seeks him." (Lamentations 3:25).

"Trust in the Lord with all your heart and do not lean on your own understanding. In all your ways acknowledge him and he will make straight your paths." (Proverbs 3:5-6)

"Behold, we consider those blessed who remain steadfast. You have heard of the steadfastness of Job and you have seen the purpose of the Lord, how the Lord is compassionate and merciful." (James 5:11)

"Wait for the Lord and keep his way, and he will exalt you to inherit the land; you will look on when the wicked are cut off." (Psalm 37:34)

"Our soul waits for the Lord; he is our help and our shield." (Psalm 33:20)

"And we know that for those who love God all things work together for good, for those who are called according to his purpose." (Romans 8:28)

Chapter 3

Two Traits That Stand Out

Many people want to get many things done but there are two traits in particular that are necessary in being an overachiever: focus and determination. You have to have both in order to be an overachiever because those are two of the qualities that cause a person to work darn hard, darn consistently and don't allow the darn distractions, naysayers or circumstances to derail them.

Could Julia have worked out with the door open? Sure. But that's not what was going to give her the focus that she needed. She needed to cut out her pet, her family, and any distractions that would have caused her to be 5% less focused. And that 5% less would have derailed her completely.

Focus and determination are particularly important because in our world, there are so many things vying for our attention. We have to have these two qualities in order to ensure that we are doing all that we can and all that we need to in order to propel ourselves to greater levels.

Focus and determination means that despite the many distractions and discouragement that can be around us, we can focus and we can work consistently and diligently on what needs to be done. It is really important to take on this can-do attitude. Some of you reading this may come from families that do not believe they can accomplish much. Good on you, therefore, for picking up this book because that tells me that you have a keen interest, desire and you will dedicate yourself to the accomplishment and attainment of your objectives.

It Doesn't Usually Happen Overnight

Overachievers are not created overnight and achievements are not accomplished overnight. Overachievers are people who have seen difficulty and have had to work really hard to overcome those difficulties and achievements don't just happen - they are things we have to work really hard at. Overachievers are people who have had to be consistent in their resolve to get something done and they have necessarily had to figure out what worked for them based on what the Holy Spirit has shown them. In the introduction, I pointed out the example of Julia on the treadmill. That may not be what everyone needs to have run longer and further and more consistently, but the common thread among all overachievers is that they have figured out what is required for them to have laser focus and they went after it with that laser focus.

You Will Encounter Obstacles

No matter what area you are looking to accomplish anything, be prepared to encounter obstacles.

What are obstacles? Obstacles are anything that happen or that threaten to happen that may derail you from what you need to do for the accomplishment of your goals. Obstacles can and will come in many different forms and ways and we often need to be creative when we think about their solutions. One of the most important things we can do when we encounter an obstacle is (you guessed it) pray for the Lord's wisdom with it. Pray for how He would guide you around that problem and then remain open to what He shows you. I said it before and I'll say it again, *"His ways are not our ways when you are dealing with things so be open to His ways"* (Isaiah 55:8-9). He sees further, wider and more completely than you do.

When I was looking to get into the school board I am currently employed with, I met many obstacles along the way. I needed to figure out how I was going to navigate everything and also balance the caregiving duties I had at home. I needed to make sure my paperwork was done perfectly, my application documents contained everything that would be needed, to ace the interview (that was also in French, by the way) and then I had to wait a long time for my paperwork to be processed and to receive an offer to be hired. It was an arduous process and was made more difficult by the fact that some reps that I had spoken to kept asking for more and more paperwork when I had already provided everything that was required. Today, I am employed by the new school board and I love being here because I get to pray with my students, I get to talk about and teach about the Christian faith and I get to explain to the kids how they can and should working with Jesus and being led by the Holy Spirit for all their needs, in addition to teaching them curriculum and how to improve in reading and in writing. I encountered many obstacles along the way but an overachiever doesn't let those obstacles keep them down and say "Ok, forget it." If you know something is important to you, you work with the Holy Spirit to figure out a way. You move on if and when the Holy Spirit tells you to, not if and when you think it's the right thing to do.

When we listen too much to the opinions of others and we don't move forward without receiving their validation, we are shooting ourselves in the foot, so to speak. Other people don't have your vision. They don't know your ultimate goals and what God has put on your heart. They are not likely to be in the same frame of mind as you to guide you the way the Holy Spirit guides you.

It is therefore so very important for overachievers (and wannabe overachievers) to focus and do you. Focus on what you need to focus on. There is nothing wrong with sometimes sharing on social media, but most people look to social media and they get highly influenced by those they see. If the people you are following are not overachievers, you aren't likely going to be influenced to be one.

Not Getting Swayed

When we work on something in a determined manner, it means that we don't allow ourselves to be swayed....by anything. We steadfastly remain focused and we steadfastly make sure that we are dedicating time, energy and resources to the successful accomplishment of this endeavor. Yes, determination means you will need to dedicate serious time to this endeavor. Yes, determination means you will need to dedicate serious resources to this endeavor. Yes, determination means you will need to dedicate serious efforts to this endeavor. Yes, determination means you will need to forego other things you could have spent that time and those resources on in order to accomplish this endeavor.

Determination also means having faith. When we have been led to something by the Holy Spirit, it doesn't mean it will be convenient and it does mean that we will have to exercise determination to the successful end as a result of our determination. Nobody who has ever accomplished anything of value ever had it easy. Life just doesn't work that way. There will always be challenges and difficulties, things that don't work our way, difficult people and circumstances and much more. If you are not dedicated to the goal and to the successful completion of the goal, you will not see it come to pass.

As ones who rely on Christ, we have an added benefit. You see, as followers of Christ, we are in consistent partnership with Christ, and that means that we are never on our own to accomplish something. It means that we rely on Christ and lean on Him for anything we have to do, making our burden and load much easier. It is also really important to realize that when you partner with Christ, you are not always subject to the physical and natural realities. For example, when a friend of mine was working on building her business, she knew she didn't have the money on her own, and neither did her family. She knew that she would need to access God's resources to get what was needed and she did. All the right people, situations and circumstances started falling into place because she had been praying and because she knew that she was in business with God.

Keeping You On Track

Another benefit to working with God and to being in partnership with Him is that you realize that He keeps you on track, when you ask Him to. Many business coaches and organizations charge high fees to be your coach, to help you stay the course, to help you figure out the best strategies. With God, you have the best Coach working in your corner, and not charging you one red cent. Instead, He looks for your (and here are those words again) focus, dedication and your resolve to follow Him.

Tuning In

Some people, even some Christians, don't know a lot about tuning in to the Holy Spirit for help, guidance and advice. One reason for this is that it isn't taught in schools and not all churches teach this. It is sometimes not even preached.

But just because we haven't been taught about it or not taught enough about it, it doesn't mean it isn't there. It doesn't mean it isn't necessary. **It just means we need to learn how to tune in to it and to see what the Holy Spirit is telling us and how to follow what He tells us.**

The way the Holy Spirit speaks to you will be personal. It will be unique in that God knows how you are and what you like (He created you) so He will be the One who knows how to reach you, how to get to your core.

My advice is to remain open to this because it is how we have been designed to do life.

Chapter 4

God At The Center

All of my books have God at their center. There is a reason: God is the Creator, the One who loves us, wants the best for us, owns everything and He will guide you to be such an awesome creator as well.

Pray for God to work on you from the inside and to make you an overachiever and one who gets things done. Pray for Him to create that within you. He will. God is with us all the time and He is the Ultimate Overachiever. He is the One who created everything and He is the One who designed the earth to be so awesome: humans, birds, nature, water, trees, love, romance, laughter, and the list really does just go on and on. He is the Ultimate Creator and we were made in His image, in His likeness. As such, we were created to be creators in our own right but because we are still humans and faulty, we need His help to become all that He created us to be. His help is accessed through prayer and He is an awesome God who delivers each time.

God has an amazing way of working within us from the inside in order to create us into beings who are capable of much more than we would if He were not working within us. He is amazing at transforming us from the inside out, if we let Him. We let Him by engaging in prayer and then seeing how the Holy Spirit changes us, moves us, lifts us, engages us, and ultimately, transforms us.

If you have never prayed to God before (for this or for anything else), now is a great time to begin. One of the best things about God is His ability to work within us even if we have never before given Him a moment of our time. He is that awesome, that forgiving, that loving. God is love and that necessarily means that anyone who comes to Him will receive from His love and His goodness. So, if you have never prayed before or you are not used to praying, may I offer this suggested prayer in an effort to have Him transform you and work in you to create in you an overachiever who works at all the right things. All the right things that He wants for you. *"Father God, I come to You through Your Son, Jesus. I ask You to change me and to create in me a person who does as per Your will and may You create in me a person who is focused, strategic, hard working and works at all the right things and in the right timing. I ask You to speak to my heart clearly through the Holy Spirit and show me the right ways. In Jesus' name. Amen"*

Stay Attuned

The Holy Spirit doesn't work within you for one day and then say "Ok, now you're all healed and good to go and do so on your own!" No, the Holy Spirit works within you a little each day to help you strive, to help you see ways and things that are there and that you and others may have missed because you and they either weren't paying attention enough or weren't attuned to God. The Holy Spirit is that still small voice inside of you that is guiding you this way or that and it is important that we take the time and demonstrate the respect needed to listen carefully and to follow what It is guiding us to do.

Many people are under the impression that we are supposed to be doing life on our own and on our own terms. I emphatically say no to that. With all due respect to my reader, we were not created to be independent from God in what we do. We were created to go through life in communion with Him and to follow His perfect will for our lives. We were created and we were and are called to follow His will for our lives because He created us, so He knows exactly what skills, talents and gifts He has put inside of us.

I cannot create a gorgeous mural or painting because that is not the skill that He has put in me. I was never meant to be a great painter like Picasso because that's not my path. That wasn't His will for me.

An example: one morning, I woke up very early and chose to sit in stillness and in quiet with the Holy Spirit. I asked Him to speak to my heart about what He wanted me to do, what direction He wanted me to take. I was led and inspired to take a certain course through a school I had barely heard of but it seemed really interesting and was a faith-based course. I had already been reading the Bible and journaling a lot at that point so taking this course didn't seem like it would be outside of my comfort zone. When my course materials arrived, I knew I was onto something special. I completed course after course, devouring the course teachings and working in a focused, strategic and resolute manner, ensuring that I was getting an A on each item I handed in by email, after having read and ensured that I understood what the course requirements were to get that "A". I worked hard and yes, I had to sacrifice and work in resolute ways but it led to my Doctorate in Prophetic Ministry. I thoroughly enjoyed each course and thoroughly enjoyed writing those long position papers. That was one of my paths the Lord had set for me.

What Is He Calling You To Do?

Have you ever thought about this? What is He calling you to do? Is He trying to get your attention to do something in particular? I can pretty much assure you that He is because He has an awesome plan for every single person. Just because you may not know Him or you don't feel close or connected to Him, it doesn't mean that He doesn't have a plan and a path for you.

How Is He Calling You To Do It?

More than one person can be called to do the same thing but it's how you are supposed to do it that might differentiate you completely from others. For example, there are many buildings that are created but how those builds are to be created are not all going to be the same. They are necessarily going to be different because God is a God of variety. He will not guide each person to do a thing in the same way, using the same design each time. He will show one person to design it this way, to approach it that way and a variety of other factors.

So the question of how He is calling you to do it is a really important question and one that I suggest you take some time to really think about and reflect on. If you attempt to do it in a way that is even a bit different from the way He has called you to do it, it will not work in the right way (the way He says).

Take this book for example. Many authors before me have written about getting it done. I know I am not the first and it is unlikely that I will be the last. But I am the only one who can and has written the book in this way, in this time and using my particular set of word choices, chapter choices and titles, length, etc. This is the way that I was called to write this book you have picked up and hopefully, it will resonate with you to do what He has called you to do, in the timing and in the way that He has called you to do so.

Many other Christian authors write spectacular books that I am very much in awe of. That's their way. I can be inspired to write in the same flavour or using certain style elements that are the same but my way is my way that He has called me to. What is yours for your passion project?

When Is He Calling You To Do It

Just as the previous questions were very important, so is this one. When is He calling you to do something? Everything has a specific time frame and if we don't do what we are called to do within the specific time frame, then we are not following His design the way that we are supposed to.

For example, if you know that you are supposed to be sending that client the quote that they asked for but you don't do it within a reasonable time frame, then you are not doing what you were supposed to do. This leads the client to conclude that you may be flaky, not trustworthy, that you are not willing to dedicate your time to their project needs, etc. It reflects very poorly on you and yes, you can technically send them the quote days, weeks or months later but they will likely have moved on and will no longer be interested in your services.

As an example to this point: I recall a contractor I was considering working with. I had asked for a simple renovation and had indicated that the budget was not grand. This contractor had an opportunity to be engaged in work and knew my parameters. He came in with another individual (I did not know the other individual would be coming) and he provided me with the most expensive quote I had ever seen, even for work I had not asked him to do and using some of the most expensive materials on the market. None of what I had asked for.

In the end, I definitely chose not to work with that contractor and never regretted my decision.

Chapter 5

Focus In Real, Everyday Terms

Just as the title suggests, we have to be focused in what we are called to do and that focus has to play out in our daily lives. This means being focused through work commitments, family commitments, and the many, many, many, many other commitments we all have. This can also mean praying for time to open up in our day so we can do what we need to do.

In practical, every day terms, this will mean:

- Taking time out each day to work on the steps required
- Motivating yourself to do the best you can through the Holy Spirit
- Praying for motivation, focus of vision and resolve
- Eliminating (not just limiting) distractions
- Not talking to everyone about your plans
- Never making excuses for not getting done what needs to be done
- When inspiration and an idea strikes, writing it down (when the title for this book came to me one night, I was

extremely stoked and immediately jotted it down on my laptop even though I was being called to dinner)
- Not thinking about other things when you are working
- Putting your best into what you are doing
- Not focusing on the mountain in front of you, but instead, focusing on the tasks in front of you and how you can do each of those extremely well

Balancing Our Time

When you are called to do something, it is important to pray on how you are supposed to calibrate your time. I know that when I began writing chapter books, I had many other demands on my time but I also knew that God does not call us to do something without giving us the tools and the means to do it. In other words, He is not a God who sets us up for disappointment. As such, we have to ask Him how we are supposed to balance our time properly:

- Is now the right time to do this?
- How do You want me to do this? What is the scope of the work?
- Am I supposed to be doing this on my own or am I supposed to be seeking/hiring help?
- Am I supposed to do all the same things as before in addition to this new task?
- How many hours am I supposed to dedicate per day, per week or per month to doing this?
- How can I manage my time so that I am ready and prepared with whatever I need to have ready and in the time frame that He is calling me to be ready?

- Do I currently have the right understanding for this project in order to do everything correctly for this?

Write Down Your Answers

Documenting and writing out the answers you believe you are getting are very important steps. They keep you on-track, accountable, and you can continually and regularly go back and keep checking on what has been done, what needs to be revised, what needs to be done, etc.

With time, memories get fuzzy. As such, we need to write things down and we need to keep track of all that was communicated to us. Even if it's just a file folder of previous emails and communications on your own notepad or device, use it for your benefit and to keep track of next steps.

One thing in particular that I do is that I write down:

1. Very detailed notes of what I needed to do and what I actually did, including how long each thing took me to do and specific responses I got from people.
2. Jot down how I felt doing it and any important tidbits of information, such as any additional thoughts that popped up, new ideas and suggestions for myself to improve myself or my project, etc.
3. Follow up dates, times and appointments I have for next steps and what specific actions need to be taken for those next steps.

For example, a friend of mine that I also wrote about in one of my previous books said that she felt led to start a business but she already had a growing family, she needed to support her husband in his business and she needed to make sure that she took time to spend alone with God because she had experienced some mental health challenges.

So, she prayed over this decision considerably. She began to see how she already had many of the pieces required in-place for her new business and that she would only need to add very little to her proverbial plate in order to make the transition to a full-fledged business. All she really needed, according to the promptings of the Holy Spirit, were a website, a contact form and a POS system. Because of her tech savvy, she was able to build all of that in less than a week and she was off and running! Today, she makes a very healthy income from only that one website and that income really helps cover their monthly home mortgage.

God is awesome!

When God Tells You To Stop

I recall having made a decision through the promptings of the Holy Spirit to not accept a certain type of work anymore. This work, the Holy Spirit showed me, was not the best and was not a suitable use of my skills. Even though I felt I was making good income from that work, the prompting was clear that I needed to stop it completely. While initially a bit sad and disappointed because all I was looking at was the loss of income, I made the decision to follow through on the promptings of the Holy Spirit and I had told those who were bringing me this work to stop doing so because I was no longer interested in pursuing that line of work. One didn't answer my email while another said that they understood and would remove me from their list and then a couple of weeks after that conversation, I received an email from that same person offering me work for a few days and the subject read: Big $$$. This was now a temptation the person was putting in front of me. I had said that I am not doing this work anymore but the email was trying to tempt me to set aside my resolve and to take this job. Having taken that work would have been a temptation that I would have fallen into. Because at this point I am generally pretty good at staying focused and sticking to what the Holy Spirit has guided me to do, I was able to ignore the email and was able to not reply, effectively turning down the work opportunity.

What am I saying?

After you have made a decision to follow the Holy Spirit and are set on your path of focus and resolve, temptations will come. It then becomes your role to turn away from those temptations and to stay focused on your particular path and course.

I only looked at this change as a loss. But I had no idea that I was going to be presented with a different income opportunity that I never would have thought of and that actually represented a more lucrative opportunity for me. I learned (once again) that God is always looking out for our best - to bring us His best!

Yes, Obedience Does Mean Sacrifice

Of course obedience means you will have to sacrifice, and that sacrifice can mean different things for different people. You cannot do everything and be everywhere at the same time and sometimes, being obedient to His guidance means that you will have to let something go for better to come along.

When Michael Phelps wanted to be the best and most decorated swimmer in the world, he talked about the laser focus required to accomplish this. He was required to swim and practice each day and he had mathematically and methodically calculated what not swimming one day was going to mean for him. He spent time visualizing and running runs over and over again in his mind and he knew psychologically the frame of mind that would be required for this incredible and yet achievable goal. Did he have to sacrifice for the attainment of this goal? You better believe it. Of course he did. He had to sacrifice tons in order to achieve this but he did and he became the most decorated Olympian of all time.

He utilized the tools I am telling you about in this book: laser focus, strategy, methodically calculating what would be needed to get this done and he stuck to it. If you waiver even a little bit from any one of these action attributes, you risk falling a little bit short from what is needed and that's not what we are looking for.

Now I also want to be very clear that we should never just set arbitrary goals for ourselves just so that we can say we are an overachiever. Definitely not. We need to be clear in:

1. What God is saying (where He is guiding us to be overachievers)
2. How we are supposed to proceed with this

3. In what time frame we are supposed to proceed with this

God Is Always Specific

One of my favorite things about God's ways is how specific He always is. He has a definite way and path to getting things done and He doesn't waiver from that. He factors in the contextual givens and He provides a way that He knows will be the best way around everything. He also always communicates that to those who ask. He is always very strategic and He always makes sure that He is guiding us to the best, fastest and most intelligent way to achieve something.

God May Not Use The Way We Think Is Best

God also is so interesting and much due respect to Him because He may not always guide you to the way that may seem so obvious to us humans. He may guide us via a pathway that is completely different but that, in the end, still achieves what it needed to achieve and in a smarter and better way than the "normal" path would have been.

We are human and our viewpoint is very limited. God is not subject to the same limitations as us and so when He guides us via a different path than the one we may think is best, we have to have blind faith and go with what He guides.

When Focusing Is A Challenge

Let's face it, sometimes being and remaining focused is a challenge. We sometimes are not sure how to get and stay focused, especially with the busy lives we all lead. But that doesn't mean that just because it can be challenging, that we shouldn't work at it and pray for help in ensuring that. When focus is a challenge, I pray through it. Here is one such suggested prayer: *"Lord, You know that I am having difficulty getting focused. You have guided me to take these actions to the attainment and fulfillment of these goals and for that, I am very grateful. Now, I need to ask You to help me get focused. Help me tune out all unnecessary distractions and help me be as focused as I need to be and for as long as I need to be so. In Jesus' name. Amen."*

When I said earlier that we were not supposed to do everything on our own, I meant that. Even getting or staying focused is something He has promised to help us with. He has promised to help us through each and every step but we have to ask for the help. Asking means that we are humbling ourselves and we are acknowledging that we are human and that we do need help. Asking means that we know and acknowledge that He is the Great, Sovereign Lord and that nothing is impossible for Him. Asking means that we are acknowledging our dependence on Him. God never turns away from someone who requires help.

So, I ask you:

1. Have you asked Him for help?
2. Have you prayed for the Holy Spirit to speak to you?
3. Have you demonstrated your reliance on His goodness and His Sovereignty?

4. Have you asked Him each morning to guide your steps?
5. Have you followed through diligently and completely on what He has guided you to do?
6. If you were not sure of the direction provided, did you pray again to ask for clarification?
7. Did you ask in what time frame are you supposed to be doing this?
8. Have you asked Him to bring to your mind any wrongs you were supposed to right or asked Him for His help in helping you right any wrongs?

Time Frames

I want to be clear about this point about time frames. God has a specific time in which something needs to be done. Even within one day, He can require something to be done at a certain time in that day, not a minute before or after. When we are tuned in to Him and to His ways, we see how important the time frame is and why something needs to be done within that particular time frame. It is really important to make sure that we are following through with His requirements because He knows things are coming that we cannot see, and He has factored those into the time frames. Chapter 5 - Resolve

Resolve means the ability to see something through to completion even though there are many difficulties and obstacles in the way. Resolve is continuing to work at something even despite all the obstacles that are in the way and working around all the issues.

When we have set a goal for ourselves as overachievers, we work tirelessly at seeing that goal through to completion. We work hard and we work strategically, ensuring that our time is very well spent and we account for each hour used. We know that each new step taken is one that has been mapped-out in our minds as essential to the completion of the task because we have forward-thought and forward-planned. Overachievers don't simply "do". They have a strategy behind each thing they do and they make sure that each item they are doing is done in the best ways possible.

For example, as the world's most decorated Olympian, Michael Phelps talks about how he carefully calculated each swim and each move within each swim. He talks about how an Olympic-level swimmer would need to think about and consider the ramifications of a day off from swimming and whether that seemingly-simple action would prove to not be beneficial enough to undertake, given that he would need more than a couple of days to reintegrate himself back into the pool after that day of swimming. He and his coach had carefully examined each move and each strategy, seeing how each thing he did would be conducive to his overall Olympic goal.

One of the amazing things about having so many great examples of overachievers in the world today and from so many different walks of life is that we can see that no matter where you came from, no matter what you have been through, no matter what your upbringing is, that you can still achieve your goals and dreams and you when you work hard and strategically, there are no limits to what you and God together can do!

Personally, I have a tremendous amount of respect for people who make the decision (yes, it is absolutely a decision) to be conscious, to be present, to work hard and to pound the proverbial pavement each day, each hour, and working to make sure that they do all that they can to attain their goals.

Setting Your Mind

Setting your mind and keeping it set does not mean you will not have moments of doubt. You will. Setting your mind means that you continue to work with resolve through those moments of doubt, and defeating that small voice that says "you can't do this" or "who do you think you are to try to achieve something like this." It means pushing through when those not-great thoughts come to our minds, and we each have those thoughts that appear.

It is a true leader who can admit that they have those moments of weakness but to say that they are still trudging through those weaknesses and working in the face of those weaknesses! Why so? Because they know that others are watching and they can see that their example is just that....an example. They are impacting the lives of others and influencing people to strive for and to reach their own dreams. All in the face of often-incredible challenges and difficulties.

When God Puts A Dream On Your Heart

It also has to be said that when God puts a dream on your heart, He isn't checking your bank account. He isn't checking that you have the financial resources to get this done. He is checking for your willingness and your availability. He is checking to see that you are willing to follow Him and to do all that He calls you to do, despite the challenges.

When my mind was bustling (in a good way) with ideas for my books, I knew that I had many interesting (at least to me) ideas for book subjects and topics. I knew that I wanted to share my faith in Christ and that I wanted my books to make a positive difference. I had already experienced being published through a traditional publisher and both what that entailed and what that would bring. I realized that that way was not for me and that I enjoyed creating and having control within my own publishing house. I also loved being online and I knew that I could work for hours upon hours at my laptop each day with all the creative pieces at hand. But I also knew that I had some tech skills I needed to pick up along the way and to figure out the layout and publishing platforms. I knew it was going to cost me money and seeing the costs of publishing and what each step and stage of the process could cost, I began praying for the Lord's wisdom on how I could get this all done within the dollars I had. Ultimately, I left the problem in its entirety to Him because I am very aware that I am only human and He is God.

One step at a time, He showed me how to undertake the many, many, many steps required for the proper and well thought-out creation of a great, whole book and I knew that if I could get that first one done, the others that follow would have a similar path. You see, as in Matthew 7:24-27, I knew that my choice would be to create my home (my publishing home in this case) upon the rock of God.

24 "Everyone then who hears these words of mine and does them will be like a wise man who built his house on the rock.
25 And the rain fell, and the floods came, and the winds blew and beat on that house, but it did not fall, because it had been found on the rock.
26 And everyone who hears these words of mine and does not do them will be like a foolish man who built his house on the sand.

27 And the rain fell, and the floods came, and the winds blew and beat against that house, and it fell, and great was the fall of it."

So, we begin. We work hard. We tailor our work and we obey Him and we listen to His wisdom. We get started and we use the lamp of God to guide our steps. Once the first step has been revealed and we follow through on it, we continue as He shows us the second step, and so on and so forth.

Keeping Yourself Accountable

When we make the decision to be overachievers and we work hard at something, we need to make sure that we are keeping ourselves accountable. In this case, that means that we document and keep track of our progress, day by day, sometimes hour by hour. For example, I keep myself accountable by reflecting on what I actually got done that day. Did I complete a chapter or two or ten? Did I format my books properly? Did I properly state Scripture and did I use Scripture in the right and proper context? Did I use the publishing platform correctly and did I select the right cover for this book?

Keeping a journal or keeping notes on your device is so important and so helpful because it tracks your progress and you can use it to journal and to ask the Holy Spirit questions about your steps (more about journaling with the Holy Spirit in the next chapter). It also helps you go back and reflect and ask the following questions:

- Did I do enough today? Yesterday?

- How can I ensure I am following the Holy Spirit in getting the right things done?
- Have I prayed through my obstacles and the challenges I am experiencing?
- Can I work more effectively for the purposes of getting more done?
- Can I work more efficiently for the purposes of getting more done?
- Am I dedicating time to things that are not important or are less important?
- What else is the Holy Spirit telling me to do? Have I started doing them?

> God is mainly looking for our availability and our dedication.

Never Heard From The Holy Spirit Before?

Now, I want to add to this section that I understand that not everyone might hear from the Holy Spirit very easily or very clearly. Some reading this may not have ever known that we as humans can hear from the Holy Spirit, and some still may have tried but have not been successful. And I understand and I empathize. This is also the right place to let you know that God is mainly looking for our availability and our dedication. This means that you do not have to have a certain career, a certain standing in life, or a certain anything to benefit from hearing from the Holy Spirit. What you need (and what He is looking for) is your willingness and your availability.

I will also state two things here: one is a prayer to invite Him to speak clearly to your heart (just below, in italics), and the other is the reminder that when you ask Him to speak, He may not do so right away or you may not recognize it yet as the voice of God. It may take a few times praying for it to happen just like it may take a few times for you to listen carefully and be able to recognize it as the voice of God.

Here is a very simple prayer to invite Him to speak to your heart:

"Jesus, I ask You to speak to my heart. I feel _____(happy, sad, confused, unsure, etc.) and I am asking You to speak to my heart about what I am going through. I am asking for Your help, Jesus. In Jesus' name. Amen "

A prayer is a deeply personal conversation between you and God and only you can decide the words you want to use to express your thoughts, desires, and what you want to talk to God about.

The next prayer is a more involved and detailed one you can use next. Remember that these prayers are only a suggested guideline. A prayer is a deeply personal conversation between you and God and only you can decide the words you want to use to express your thoughts, desires, and what you want to talk to God about. A prayer can be done in your mind or can be said out-loud - both methods are effective for prayer.

"Lord Jesus, I come to You today to ask You humbly to speak to me. I long/would like to hear from Your Holy Spirit to lead me, to guide me, to show me the way and to help me see what I need to see. I would like to begin the process and the practice of journaling, Lord Jesus, so I ask You to allow me to hear clearly from the Holy Spirit so that I may begin journaling. In Jesus' name. Amen."

Here is the process I find most helpful to hear from God through the Holy Spirit:

Step 1 - Sit in a comfortable space with no distractions (or the least number of distractions)
Step 2 - Tune in to the Lord and ask Him in your mind to speak to you
Step 3 - Pay attention to any words, thoughts, and images that come spontaneously into your mind
Step 4 - Tune in carefully to see the words, thoughts and images that come to your mind and look at them carefully. Like when you are looking with a magnifying glass, try to look at the details as carefully as possible
Step 5 - Write down / draw all that you see

You don't need qualifications to talk to God. Just talk to Him. Just pray. You only need an open heart to talk to Him.

When it comes to your illustrations: I want to note here that you don't need to be a great illustrator to write down all that needs to be drawn. Just do your best with this. What's important here is that you are writing and drawing out everything you see, feel and hear down and that you are doing it as carefully and with as much detail as possible.

When you are done, ask the Holy Spirit to talk to you again and to let you know if you have written everything correctly or if there are details you have missed. It is important to undertake this step as well because anytime we journal, we could potentially be leaving something important out and that is not a good idea. Each detail the Holy Spirit (also known as the Counselor, among His many other names) provides is important and needs to be taken note of.

Journal Checking

I would be remiss if I did not advise you to have your journal checked and in general, to see Godly counsel. Scripture states in many different places that we are to have advisors who will be there to assist us and who want God's best for us and for the people they serve. This is why it is a good idea to have Christian counselors who can ready and available to help us by praying with us and for us, by pointing out and highlighting Scripture to us and by looking over our journaling to let us know if their spirit believes that it is the Holy Spirit speaking to us and not just us being deceived or writing out our own thoughts and desires.

Here are some Scriptural passages that state the importance of doing this:

Proverbs 12:15
"The way of a fool is right in his own eyes,
But a wise man is he who listens to counsel."

Proverbs 11:14
*"Where there is no guidance the people fall,
But in abundance of counselors there is victory."*

Proverbs 13:10
*"Through insolence comes nothing but strife,
But wisdom is with those who receive counsel."*

Proverbs 15:31-33
*"He whose ear listens to the life-giving reproof
Will dwell among the wise.
He who neglects discipline despises himself,
But he who listens to reproof acquires understanding.
The fear of the Lord is the instruction for wisdom,
And before honor comes humility."*

Chapter 6

Journaling With The Holy Spirit

What does journaling with the Holy Spirit mean?

It's like when you have a pen pal that you communicate with, you write and then they write. Journaling with the Holy Spirit is no different. The Bible calls it "the indwelling Holy Spirit" (1 Corinthians 3:16) is when God's Spirit takes up residence within the person. We have His Spirit within us. Therefore, the Holy Spirit is always present and we just need to tap into that presence.

You can do this journaling on any device or even a piece of paper. You can write out your questions, comments, feelings, suspicions, etc., and the Holy Spirit will reply, help, comfort, warn and guide.

As you may be able to see, when we journal with the Holy Spirit, we are the recipient of a great gift. The Holy Spirit is God's Spirit and It shows us truth, explains things to us and Is an invaluable resource which God knew we would need. When we journal with the Holy Spirit, we are literally accessing the mind of God and there is nothing greater. Journaling helps us keep track of what God said, of steps we need to take, and helps us document things. With time, memories and exactly "what was said" can get a little fuzzy. As such, we have been provided with the Holy Spirit who is there to help us through. Journaling is one beautiful way to do this.

Journaling can and often does look different from person to person. This is generally because God has a special relationship with each of us and likes to treat us as individuals. He knows that Jeremy likes to talk to Him in one way, whereas Dillan likes to talk to Him in another, while Phoebe and Rina like to talk to Him in yet totally different ways. He knows each of us extremely well and each of us personally. He created every one of us and it is really important to factor in that when you talk to Him and journal with Him, to be as honest and as forthcoming as possible. Because God loves us so much, He always wants the best for us, so when He put His Spirit into us (which we receive after baptism), He did it with the full intention of always being there for us and with us, guiding us in the ways that only He knows how. This means that when He guides you, He has already factored in everything about you: your tastes, your ways, your likes and dislikes, your habits, your thoughts, your dreams and desires, and much more.

Each person has special callings on their lives. Every single one of us. Some peoples' callings may seem the same or similar to that of others but they are not because no two people are exactly alike and no two people have the exact same calling.

So, in a book about getting it done and being an overachiever, we have to factor in our differences in how we each get things done. In other words, I will get things done in one way while you (the reader) will get things done in a different way. But this book not only mentions those awesome and important differences (which make us each wonderfully unique) but also highlights our collective sameness because some of the same "getting it done" concepts apply to all of us. For example, focus is a skill that applies to every person, in every endeavor. What that focus looks like to person x versus person y may look different. I'll provide an example here:

Dave and Joey are both writing screenplays. They both have the wonderful God-given gift of being able to sit down, put God-given & inspired ideas to paper and work on their screenplays. As such, they will both have the task of working on their screenplays but the way they each focus on their work might look really different. Dave might need total silence and to pray before he starts to work on the next block section he has set as a goal for himself, while Joey works best and focuses best by playing loud rock music on his device because that helps him get into the frame of minds of the characters that he is writing about.

Example of Journaling

I would like to provide an example of focus journaling that was provided by Julia, a lady who is new to journaling but felt compelled to provide her example in an effort to help others better understand journaling. Here is Julia's journaling (taken with permission):

Julia: Holy Spirit, hello. I need some help getting focused today.
H.S.: Yes, talk to Me. How can I help you with this?

Julia: What do You think I should make a priority task for today? I am feeling the need to work on designing my puzzles today.

H.S.: Indeed your puzzles task is very important and inspired by Me. It is important for you to be working on that. What do you have questions about with this?

Julia: I'm not sure how to get started today and what God wants me to design with this one. I need some help getting started.

H.S.: Puzzles are amazing pastimes for so many people and very important to work on. It is worthwhile work and you are being compensated well for doing it, which is also really important. I am giving you an image in your mind right now about the design of your puzzle. It is really important for you to put this puzzle together using the exact schema I am giving you and using the exact color scheme I am giving you. This will make your puzzle extremely visually appealing which is something many people look for.

Julia: Thank You, Holy Spirit. What else should I know about creating this?

H.S.: Take your time with it. Sometimes, Julia, you feel like rushing through things. Please don't. Take your time with this and do it as best as you can, asking Me for help and for guidance throughout. Listen carefully and be open as I guide your hand in creating this puzzle and in using the specific details, highlights and more that I give you. This is the best way to make it because I know how to make this the very best puzzle for you and for those who will use it and enjoy it.

Julia: This is wonderful, Holy Spirit. Thank you. I am very excited about this.

H.S.: My pleasure.

Julia: Is there anything else I need to know about this?

H.S.: Yes, and good that you asked. I am going to speak to your heart about all the things you need to add and business pieces you need to put in place for this puzzle and your puzzles in general to be a grand success. I will speak to your heart about these and make sure to write down the things I am leading you to, sweetheart.

Julia: Thank You, Holy Spirit. I will.

It's TeamWork

Working with the Holy Spirit in getting things done is teamwork. You have a part to play, as does the Holy Spirit. You have actions to take and faith that will carry you there and so does the Holy Spirit. People who listen to the Lord for their guidance and direction are building their proverbial house on the rock, and not on the sand. When you build on the rock, you are building on the strength of God, Who is able to see all and know all, so He can advise you and guide you accordingly. This is why we say that following Him is the smartest because He knows and sees all.

When we feel led to follow a certain direction by the Holy Spirit, we have to be wise enough to follow it. This means that we need to make sure that we are following each step as it is provided to us because each step is important and the next step will rely on the successful completion of the first step.

Like I said further up, it also requires discipline and keeping our eyes open to new opportunities, new ventures and new ways. If we don't have our eyes open, we are going to miss what God is trying to put in front of us to help us. If we are not listening and attuned to God's ways, we are not putting our best in because that means that He is doing His part in the partnership but we aren't doing ours.

Journaling As Often As You Need

I want to state here that you are encouraged to journal as often as you need to. Journaling is a free activity, can be done anytime, anywhere, and in any way. You can be in the pool swimming and for a quick moment, journal something on your smartphone. You can be in the middle of a meeting and an idea pops up which you should jot onto your laptop. You can be driving somewhere and when it is safe to do so, write out that little idea that comes to you that may not immediately (at the moment) make sense but will later upon further reflection.

When I was writing my first book on a tiny piece of paper I just happened to have near my bed many years ago, I didn't know what I was writing. I didn't know I was writing the words to my first book, as He wanted my first book to be. And I definitely didn't know that upon later revision, that the words would actually make a lot of sense and would be a way to honor the Lord and all that He does for us. My first book was always meant to be a love note from God to people - His way of letting people know that He loves us and that He is inviting each and every one of us into relationship with Him.

This kind of revelation comes through journaling! Questions, Questions, Probing, Probing

God is ready and available to answer our questions and we are invited to ask, ask, ask, ask, question, ask and probe. This is something I learned the hard way when I realized that I hadn't asked enough questions about something and when things took an unfortunate turn, I asked God why He didn't tell me about that and the reply was simply: you didn't ask.

So, I learned to ask, ask, ask again, probe, probe and probe again. Even if you think you have understood something, asking again and checking again is not a bad idea. God is patient and invites us to come to Him with lots of questions. As such, we have to ensure that we are doing our part and accessing the greatest Mind in the world....to our benefit and advantage and to ensure that we are doing our part because you can be sure that God has, is and always will do His part.

Interference

Just like when we are listening to the radio and the signal isn't clear so we cannot hear things clearly, the same can happen here. Our access to hearing God can sometimes come through a bit fuzzy and it may take some time and some prayers for this interference to clear up. Why does this happen? Because the darkness does not want us to benefit from hearing from God. So we have to pray through this and push through this.

How do we do that? Simply pray. Here is a suggested prayer that can help in this case: *"Lord Jesus, I know that You are trying to talk to me. You are trying to answer my questions and lead me to Your best. You know that I am experiencing interference and that I want to be able to hear from You clearly. I ask that You help to clear up this confusion and to help me hear from You as clearly as possible. I put my trust in You and want to hear from You as clearly as I can because I am relying on Your guidance and Your wisdom through all that I am doing. In Jesus' name. Amen"*

Praying a prayer like that will alert God to the fact that you are trying to follow Him and that you are looking to do His awesome will. After all, just like with the proverbial staircase, we do need to take the first step before we get to the second step and if we have not taken the first step properly, then we are not going to successfully take the second because the next steps will be revealed to us once we have completed the first.

Chapter 7

Visualize With The Help Of The Holy Spirit

Visualizing means seeing something as done in the eyes of your heart, and having this be led by the Holy Spirit. The Holy Spirit is the One who is going to show us what God wants to bring us, when, how and what it will look like.

This is never something we have to force. This is never something we have to make happen in our own strength. It is necessarily done by the Holy Spirit because it is God's Spirit that wants to show us what God wants to bring to come to pass in our lives.

In order to do this properly, we simply have to ask the Holy Spirit to do this and we have to be attuned to what He is showing us. We are also welcome to ask many questions, ask for clarifications, and ask any questions we may have about any and all parts of this. Listening and being carefully attuned to what the indwelling Holy Spirit is saying to us and how we are being guided is both free and invaluable!

When the Holy Spirit shows us an image or a visual, take the time to stay on it and see it for all that it is. It is a clear visual He is bringing you for the purposes of communicating that He wants to bring this to you and that there are things that need to be done for this to come to you.

Therefore, this requires strategic and obedient action.

I would like to note here that there is a big difference between visualizing with the Holy Spirit and new age visualizing. NA visualizing only depends on you and has nothing to do with Jesus or the Holy Spirit. It is a means of focusing on something you want, not on something the Holy Spirit is guiding you to, and that thing may not be a good thing for you to ultimately have in your life. I should know, I used the technique in the past and it led to total disaster which I quickly had to move to remove from my life.

The visualizing I am referring to here also means that we need to focus the eyes of our hearts on Jesus. We can go to our special spot with Him, a spot where we can spend time in quiet meditation with Him and where He can show us His love for us, we can feel that love and we can act on the action items He guides us to.

When we visualize a little each day, we begin to focus more and more on the picture we are trying to get closer to and we feel "miraculously" inspired to take the actions we sense will be needed to move toward that goal and picture. This means that He will show us the steps required and yes, it is a very good idea (in fact, necessary) to continually check in with the

Holy Spirit to make sure that we are following the right path, according to Him.

When we use a vision board that is inspired by the Holy Spirit, we are using a wonderful tool to keep our goals and dreams in front of us. This means that we see it regularly and our mind begins to think about and work out how we are going to achieve this. It is such a great tool to use and keeping Jesus' name and/or the cross front-and-center is a great way to ensure that we are keeping Jesus in honor and that we are focusing on what He is guiding us to and not just what we think would be a good idea for ourselves.

Find Images From Anywhere

A vision board needs to use images that have been inspired by the Holy Spirit and the images can be from anywhere. You don't need to spend a lot of money on this.

Personalize it completely and as you work on it, focus on what the Holy Spirit said to you during your journaling. Focus on the specific guidance and the images, and look for images that most closely correspond to those goals and those specific pieces of guidance.

One thing I noticed about creating vision boards is that they can pretty frequently change and evolve. I remember I had written a dollar amount on one board I made and then a week and a half later, I changed the dollar amount. I used one image of the name of Jesus and then a few days later, found an image I liked better. As long as your vision board pieces are inspired by the Holy Spirit, you will be on the right track in terms of putting your images up.

A vision board is also a tremendous tool for staying focused and somehow makes the process of sacrificing for those goals more palatable. A vision board helps keep our target in place in our minds.

What Happens If You Realize You Made A Mistake

I don't know about you but I have made some errors in what I felt the Holy Spirit leading me to. I began focusing on the wrong thing and only realized it months later when I went deeper in prayer and realized my error. I felt at that point that turning it around would be too late but when I asked the Lord for His wisdom, He showed me how I had been on the wrong track with that particular thing for months and that now we were going to have to shift gears and fix months and months of wrong moves. It was a very humbling moment but one I am glad happened because it is better to realize your error and begin correcting it as soon as possible than to ignore the problem and keep going in the wrong direction. I am grateful to this day (years later) that I stopped, realized my error and changed direction. As of this book's writing, I am still in the process of fixing the error but I know I am on the right track and am making my way diligently to where I was supposed to be.

Daily Focus On Your Visuals

Spending time each day focusing on your visuals and your images is necessary. It helps us focus, brings those goals to the forefront of our mind, causes us to think about our goals again and it helps make the images real to us, ultimately helping us move steadily toward their achievement.

As visual creatures, humans respond very favorably to visuals and images,which means that we process images much more quickly and relate to them much more meaningfully than we do words. This is one of the many reasons God provides us with these images through His Spirit - it has the intent of making sure that we are able to best understand the image(s) and see the details that are included. When we look carefully at the images that we are provided and we can even ask questions in our minds to more clearly see the images, that is direct guidance from God about what we are supposed to be looking for and what we are supposed to be finding.

Every Person Has Their "Meant For's"

Every person has their calling, their meant fors and things that are for them. Meaning, specifically for them. I will say that other books may say that because it's for you, nobody else can have it. That is simply not true. Someone else can have it but they are not meant to. So we have to stay tuned into God and what He is guiding us to so that we can make sure that we are working toward what is meant for us.

To provide an example: years ago, I was looking for a relationship and I got influenced by a friend to go online and find someone. I found someone alright. He seemed great - charming, kind, funny, extremely good looking and so much more. Until I found out years later that he only seemed great but that he had been unfaithful and that he had been lying to me. When I prayed about this and I asked the Lord why He had brought this deceptive man to me, He replied very simply and matter-of-factly that He was not the One who had brought him to me.

We have to be attuned to God and to His prompts in order to get what is meant for us.

Chapter 8

Strategic, Inspired, Consistent Action

Our actions and our steps are so important.

We cannot get to where we need to be without them and we cannot accomplish important things without action. Actions, in order to be truly demonstrative of our talents and in order to really overachieve, need to be consistent. Yes, this does mean that we are not supposed to be doing actions only one day, one week or one month and then nothing again after that.

I also warn here that action in and of itself is not enough. It isn't wise. **Our actions need to be strategic, inspired and consistent.** In other words, when you pray for His direction and to know what to do, we have to ask for what His best advice and guidance is for strategic, inspired and consistent action. I will tackle each of the headings one at a time:

Strategic - there is a specific way in which actions need to be undertaken. We must ask God what actions are required and how we are supposed to move toward our goals, asking clarifying questions as we move forward.

Inspired - any good action that is taken has to be inspired by Him. When we wait for His guidance, we are building our home on the rock that is Him and not on sand. Tumultuous times will come but if we have followed Him properly, we will not get thrown for a loop and a half when it comes.

Consistent - we cannot take action for a day or two or ten and then think that we are done. We have to be consistent. Now, this does not mean that you will consistently do the same things over and over again, consistently. No. It means you will consistently do as He guides and when He guides you to do it.

It all comes back to relying on Him because again, you are in partnership with Him. You are not supposed to do this alone (and this can mean anything you are called to do).

People who do not work with God actually make their lives a million times harder because they are going it alone, relying only on their own human minds to accomplish things. This is unwise. Since we have the greatest Partner in the world with His wisdom, insight, control and much more at our disposal, why would we not tap into that?

I won't lie. It takes stamina to keep going at the levels of an overachiever. We have to have tremendous discipline for all of this. This could mean waking up consistently at 4 am to get your work done before work or before your kids wake up. It could mean restricting yourself from fun things that you would normally love to do. It could mean not permitting yourself certain luxuries so that you have enough to afford your latest venture.

That's why I say it takes stamina. Grit and determination are also words that come to mind and that cause us to really appreciate the value of a job well done when all is said and done.

Breaking It All Down

Overachievers have a consistent habit of breaking down all the parts and pieces of what needs to be done for their consistent success. They know that abc needs to be done on Monday because that needs to be ready for Tuesday. Macro thinkers think even more long-term and big picture and these are certainly necessary (and admirable) qualities to have. When I knew I wanted to create a certain number of new titles in one year, I broke it down into realistic chunks and I asked myself, "How many hours do I need to work per day in order to complete this book by this date?" I asked myself this question because I knew I wanted to complete a certain number of items in one year and so I had to break down that goal into realistic, manageable pieces. Doing so also helped me realize that it wasn't enough to just write 2 pages in that one day - that was not going to get me to my desired finished product and goal in the time frame I knew I wanted to meet and that I felt God led me to. So, I had to shift priorities, do a little less of something else and spend the time working on that goal. I had to put more time into it because I knew that I had a deadline to meet.

Of course, people can work on things leisurely and keep extending their deadlines again and again. But that is not what overachievers tend to do. Overachievers will do what it takes to meet their deadline because they know that not meeting it will mean that they have performed less than what was necessary.

Olympic athletes, for example, know that they have to get in a certain number of hours of practice per day and that if they don't, they are short-changing themselves. Do they get sick? Yes. Do they have days where they don't feel like training? You bet. Do they have days where they would have preferred sleeping in and taking it easy? I bet they have had those days. But being an overachiever and getting it done means you kick yourself in the behind and you push yourself to that extra 10%, 20%, 30% or whatever percentage you are in need of.

It means putting in the time and the effort even though you don't feel like it because you know you will be right back there tomorrow, again, swimming those laps, improving your game, making sure you do the course in less time tomorrow than you did today and much more. And please don't think this is limited to sports. You have great writers who push themselves to greater results each day. You have great doctors and surgeons who review their medical procedures and see how they can make things work much better next time and what materials will they need to do that. You have great teachers and lawyers and firefighters and project managers who push themselves past their working hours and they see how they can do better next time, how they can improve their last numbers and move the entire industry (not just themselves) forward. They are examples to others because they don't just work for their own benefits but the benefit of others who can see their examples, learn from them and be inspired by them!

Looking Around & Asking Questions

When we strive for better, it is sometimes wise to look around and ask questions. We can ask those who do better or who are more senior how they did that and why they did it that way. We can look at someone whose times are more impressive than our own and they look to see how they can shave time off of their performance. They look around and they ask smart questions which will lead them to a better overall performance and they make sure that they don't stop until they have performed better.

Overachievers are very smart and strategic in that way. They know that inspiration is out there and that others came before them so they know to learn from those others and to see how things can be improved. Think about it: if you are the very first in the industry to do something, you have very little if any previous data to go on, meaning that you will have to do a lot of the leg work and primary research on your own in order to have a base for comparison and improvements.

We should therefore be very grateful to all those who came before us and tried and failed or tried and succeeded. We stand on their shoulders and learn from them and overachievers make sure that they find ways to do better, go further, go faster and make that difference.

Pushing Past Disappointments

Yes, we will experience disappointments. Everyone does. Some people unfortunately get bogged down in their disappointments and they decide to quit. Others, facing those same disappointments, say that they will look harder, look more deeply and see what went wrong and will go for more, higher and better.

Which type of person are you committing to be today?

Chapter 9

Documenting

One of the best things to do to help ourselves is to document our actions and progress. Write down what you have been doing so that you can keep track and keep yourself accountable. When we write things down, we get to see:

- How each little action feeds the big accomplishment picture
- How we have honored God by following His instructions daily
- How we have shown our dedication to this endeavor by working hard and smart on this
- How we have been consistent in our steps
- What we got done that day and what needs to be carried over to the next day
- Have you accomplished all that was needed in that day
- Notes about your steps (ex. Today, I spoke to this person and this is how that brought me forward)
- Helps keep you motivated and proud of yourself

Documenting does not have to look fancy. Not at all. But documenting does have many benefits and since you are looking to overachieve, we need to be sure that we are doing our very best to document as accurately as possible. This necessarily means that you need to take into account all that you did and did not do in a day.

You need to document in the ways that work best for you. That could mean taking notes on paper while riding the subway or jotting down details on your smartphone and then adding new details to your calendar. It could look like touching base with your best friend and seeing any other suggestions he or she may have. It could look like quiet time with God to see if He says you are on the right track and then writing that down to make sure you are documenting that He said that and then how He guides you after that.

"Christine, I Don't Know How To Hear From the Holy Spirit"

Many people report this and I understand that and respect people who say so because they are being honest. I too did not hear properly until one day I did. Hearing from the Holy Spirit is an art but it is available to everyone. To aid anyone who does not feel they are hearing at all or hearing well, here is a list of all that praying will require:

- Praying for and asking Him to speak to you clearly and directly
- Quiet time spent alone with God
- Focus on any inclinations, feelings, and spontaneous auditory promptings
- Asking direct, specific questions

- Asking Him to speak to you in any way that He wants
- If you know you have things to repent for, repent for those things and then ask Him again

Document Successes

When I was looking to complete my first limited edition film project, I put up little reminders for myself all around my living space reminding me to take consistent action, to work hard and diligently at what the Lord had guided me to do and I celebrated my little wins along the way (more on celebrating little wins just below).

I put reminders for myself around my living space of the tasks that needed to be done, notes of encouragement for myself and a vision of the completed task that made sense to me. In these ways and using these tools, I was able to consistently remind myself of what needed to be done, I encouraged myself that I was working in faith, I consistently reminded myself that I am doing a great job following His will and then a lovely visual for myself of the task completed, which made me feel that sense of accomplishment each time I saw it.

I felt really great about this because I had put reminders for myself everywhere of not only what was to be done (and congratulating myself for each step) but also what the completion of the tasks looked and felt like!

Now, this is a way that worked for me. It does not mean it will necessarily work for you but it is important to put in place the documentation practices that do work for you.

Another great tool is to use a scrapbook. A scrapbook is a book where you can write out your daily, weekly, monthly, etc., accomplishments and let's say if you are living with people and don't want them to see your documentation practices, you can use this method because it is like a diary - people should not be opening it without your consent.

Celebrating The Little Wins

One of my favorite things to do is to celebrate the little wins along the way. Little wins are exactly what it sounds like - you are celebrating something good or an accomplishment along the way. It can be something as simple as you managed to send out that difficult email or you made an important appointment that will ultimately be leading to you making a great new contact or moving forward in your project. Whatever it is, it is a wonderful opportunity for you to celebrate steps in the right direction.

Accomplishing goals takes time and lots of consistent effort. One way to make this journey and process easier and more pleasant is to celebrate having taken a step, and then another, and then another, and so on and so forth. This helps to "break up" the workload in your mind and helps you realize that all will not be done in one day, one week or one month. It's a great reminder that we need to stay the course in a slow and steady manner because we are setting ourselves up for disappointment if we are not factoring in that great goals will take lots of time and effort.

I can tell you from my own experience that celebrating the little wins made things more palatable and easier to handle.

For example, when I would finish all the writing I wanted to do that day, I would celebrate by enjoying a snack with my family or a phone call with a friend that would put me in a good mood and where I could talk about the efforts I had just made.

Staying Organized

When you are trying to accomplish great things, it is vital to stay organized. We have paperwork, communications, agreements and much more that will only get muddled and jumbled if we do not take time to keep them organized.

As such, creating file folders and keeping all papers organized is vital. That organization can and will look different from person to person and will require you to be consistent at getting and keeping organized.

Writing down meeting dates and information and agenda items are also important and go a long way in ensuring that you are (and appear) professional and on-the-ball.

The last point I would like to make about documentation is that as you are going through all of these steps, disappointments will come. Rude people and naysayers will come. Don't let them get you down.

I remember I was meeting with two ladies for committee work. I sensed that they were being less than respectful and were putting down the work I was doing. It took a lot for me to continue working with them and to push past those rude remarks. There is a big difference between criticism and constructive criticism. Constructive criticism is when a person has your (or the organization's best interests at heart) and they are providing you with helpful, respectful feedback in order to help you get better. Criticism is just a person being rude and disrespectful about what you have done and putting down your work. I remember I had reached out to the project manager in the committee work and she was just talking away while she was typing and working on other things, not really thinking about what she was saying and just babbling away, not even really listening to my points of objection. I felt not heard and very disrespected and had to pray through what to do. At times, that can be an indication that you are not in the right place and that this is not for you, and at other times, it can be an indication that you need to assert yourself more and to stand up for yourself.

Sometimes, you may not have a chance to move away from those rude people or naysayers and in that case, I would advise you to pray about how the Holy Spirit suggests you move forward. There is always a solution to a problem - you may just not be seeing it yet or it may be a solution you don't really like but it is still a solution and a lifeline.

Chapter 10

Eliminate Hurtful, Harmful, Detrimental Thoughts As Much As Possible

Hurtful, negative and derogatory thoughts will come. We all experience them and they will often come completely out of the blue. These are the thoughts that put you down, make you doubt yourself, tell you that you're not good enough, that you will never accomplish what you need to and so on and so forth. We all experience them and they are unpleasant to say the least.

So, what do we do when these thoughts come? How do we deal with them? How do we silence them and help ourselves continue to move forward, despite sometimes feeling like we can't?

We have to work to tune them out. This means that we as people can choose where we give our time and our attention. We can choose which empowering thoughts we will listen to or which disempowering thoughts we will listen to. We can also select which empowering people we will keep in our surroundings and which disempowering people we will keep in our surroundings.

Praying Bad Thoughts Away

I get asked quite often if we can pray bad thoughts away. The answer is certainly yes. The Lord can shield us from bad thoughts and can help us stay positive despite things going on in the world or around us.

Here is a suggested prayer for this (again, you can change the words to suit your context and your life):

"Jesus, I pray for You to help me by taking away the negative and detrimental thoughts I am experiencing. You know why these thoughts are coming and You know how to shield me from these. I am asking You to shield me and to protect me from these negative thoughts and to speak to my heart about them. I pray for Your protection today and each day, Jesus, and to help me see anything that I need to see. In Jesus' name. Amen"

A young man that I know didn't seem to me to be doing very well. He seemed to be struggling quite a bit and seemed to be off-track. When he spoke, I sensed that there was an effort to speak, to share, and he generally seemed unhappy and unsure of himself. I wanted to cautiously know a little more about this young man not for the purposes of judging him, but so that I would know what to say when I prayed for him. As time went on and I continued to see him, things didn't seem to be getting better and then I discovered that he was badly in debt. Following that, I found out that he had gotten involved in illegal drugs. I also knew that he was taking anti-depression medication and so I wondered how his anti-anxiety medication was going to be interacting with his illegal drug use. I then looked at the company he kept. The people around him were, as I came to discover, addicted to drugs, badly in debt, heavy partiers and those who lacked direction, guidance and motivation to do better in life.

The people we choose to have in our lives matter.

It matters whom we choose to keep company with because the people around us will influence us, whether we want them to or not and whether we think they are or not. When they speak about their future and they take strategic action, we will undoubtedly be inspired to do the same. Conversely, if we associate with people who are unmotivated and make poor choices, that too will influence us.

People who are very motivated and are go-getters tend to associate with like-minded people, who also push them into setting higher, greater and better standards for themselves. People who allow themselves to get caught up with and be influenced by others who lack motivation will eventually be influenced to do the same.

Now, I want to be clear that just because one may not have resources aplenty does not qualify as "less-than". Your starting off point may not be the best but what matters is what you do with it. If you choose to stay in a less-than-ideal space, then you allow that standard for yourself. I am a very firm believer that anyone can pull themselves out of a bad situation and can strive for better in their lives.

When I began writing, it never dawned on me to write many books. I intended to write a few books and that was it. Until the Lord got a hold of me and put it on my heart to strive for better - and to write and write and write by giving me idea after idea after idea. He also brought extremely prolific authors to my mind who had written hundreds and hundreds of books and I began to expand my mind about what was possible and to strive for better. That idea didn't come from me - it came 100% from the Lord. I just obeyed and decided to make the time in my life (and to discipline myself) to follow through on what I felt I was being prompted to do.

Did the negative thoughts come to me, telling me I was nuts for even thinking I could write, publish and sell that many books? Certainly. But as I am advising you to do today, I pushed those thoughts away. I pushed those thoughts to the trash pile and decided not to listen to them. I also made (and make) it a practice to pray through those negative, disempowering thoughts. I ask God to help me by taking away those thoughts and to replace them with wonderful, empowering thoughts that will propel me to greater. Here is a suggested prayer for doing this:

"Lord Jesus, I need Your help. You see, hear and know of the bad thoughts that come to me. I need Your help in pushing those thoughts out and away from me. I need Your help in making those thoughts go away and not return. I pray for Your help in trying to do better in life and to getting me to a better place in my life. I thank You in advance for Your help. In Jesus' name. Amen"

I also want to note here that even if you don't think of yourself as a praying Christian, that you can still benefit from the prayers presented in this book. What you are doing with each prayer is asking God for help and God does not have a habit of turning people away who genuinely ask for His help....or His forgiveness.

The Practice Of Positive Self-Talk

In Proverbs 18:21, we see the verse: *"Life and death are in the power of the tongue, and those who love it will eat its fruit."* The Bible is showing us how important our thoughts are but also the importance of our words. When we speak positive words over our lives, we are literally bringing more life onto us. When we speak negative words over our lives, we are literally bringing more death onto us. When we bring life onto us, we are saying good, empowering, positive things about ourselves, making it more likely for us to propel ourselves to better, to greater and to higher levels. Speaking negatively will have the same effect but in reverse.

Here are some examples of positive words followed by some examples of negative words. I am including both here so that you can see the subtle differences and you can choose which you would like to use for yourself and for access to God's best for you or not.

Positive words: I am wonderful and have a sound mind, body and soul. God made me in His wonderful image.
Negative words: I am a total loser. Nothing good has ever happened to me and nothing good ever will.

Positive words: I am capable, through Christ, of doing incredible things and I rely on the Lord to show me how He wants me to accomplish those incredible things.

Negative words: I can't do anything right. My _____ was right - I will never amount to anything.

Positive words: If I dedicate the time and work hard and strategically on this, I can accomplish anything.

Negative words: I will never get this right. I am a complete failure at everything I do.

As you can see, the thoughts we entertain and the words we speak matter. They don't just matter to ourselves, but they also matter to others. You never know who is watching, listening and paying attention. Therefore, it is really important how you choose to spend your time - choose to empower yourself through Christ and choose to empower others as well.

Learn From The Good Examples & The Bad Ones

As the sub-heading indicates, we can learn a lot from bad examples as well as good examples. We can learn from bad examples because they are there and designed to show us what we don't want and how we should not be. As an example: a woman I used to know (who was brilliant and very intelligent) consistently doubted herself and would never allow herself to strive for better in life. She often spoke of having lofty dreams of being a great attorney and I felt strongly that this would be such a wonderful path for her. Her family was from a meager financial situation and so she wondered how she would be able to pay for law school. I asked her about the current job she had and how she had previously told me how well it paid. When she brought up the tuition fee concern, I reminded her of her current job and asked her if she was making enough to cover the tuition cost. She explained that actually, because she lived at home and had no major expenses, that she would be able to put all the money toward law school. The financial factor didn't seem to be such an issue anymore. But she was unable to motivate herself to put all the little pieces together to accomplish what she had wanted. She failed to be decisive in her actions not only toward law school but toward any career, ultimately causing her to not pursue anything.

On the other hand, a young man I knew and grew up with also came from meager beginnings, as his family didn't have much. But he worked very hard, He stayed late at the library every night, he poured over those law books like nobody else, he worked on his discussion questions so that in class, he would be able to stand out and be considered for an unpaid internship by his professor, he worked extremely hard and extremely diligently at ensuring he did absolutely everything he needed to do to get himself to where he needed to be. Today, he is one of the top attorneys in all of Toronto and continues to work extremely diligently to make the money he desires and to be at his best for his clients who rely extremely heavily on his expertise in all ways.

What is the difference between these two individuals? One did not allow themselves to be side-tracked, to let their past hold them back, to allow themselves to be anything less than completely focused on what he needed to do. The other hummed and hawed for years.

Now, I am not saying that one cannot have some time to mull things over and to decide which path is the right path. We all need that time. But what is really important to differentiate here is that one must make their decision and then go after it extremely diligently. That is what being an overachiever is all about.

Chapter 11

The Inconvenient

Yes, being an overachiever sometimes means you will get up at 4 am with an inspired thought or action item that you want to perform. Those are strategic, God-inspired moments of greatness and you would be wise to jot down the ideas. You see, God often speaks to us in quiet and in stillness. We are not frequently more quiet or more still than when we are sleeping so it does make sense that we might wake up at 4 am with an inspired thought or idea.

Overachievers are thinking, processing and mentally rehearsing virtually 24/7. And that's not a bad thing. Overachievers get so excited about what they have to do that they sometimes either can't sleep or they wake up super early with their hearts and minds jostling with buzz-worthy thoughts, ideas they can't wait to jot down or put into practice and strategies they believe will work very well in the accomplishment of their desires.

When I woke up that morning when I had decided to enroll in the first course of my Doctorate program, I was nervous and excited and I emailed the school very early in the morning.

Sure, the administrator may not have gotten back to me right away but that's besides the point. I had sent that email and I was excited about the first steps. I sent my email and I knew that she would get back to me when she did, meaning that I knew that I was setting things in motion in the right ways. I didn't have a person pushing me, encouraging me to do that or anything of the sort. I had God who put that desire and that fire in my heart and I chose to follow through. Did I have other things to do with my day? Sure. Did I wonder if I would have the financial means to make the tuition payments? Sure. Did I wonder if I would have the time to complete all the course work and do so within the time frames required by the university? Sure. But I also kept in mind that where God leads, He provides. I had enough faith to know that I would be able to do this ONLY with His guidance and His help.

Back to my example about Michael Phelps - you cannot spend that much time dedicated to swimming and that many hours in the pool without being dedicated to the practice and to the process. There is an excited energy that comes with these things that propels you to focus, to sacrifice, to getting done each individual step in the way that it needs to be done.

Here are some more examples of challenges, difficulties, addictions and inconveniences but that the person persevered through:

- A woman I know was trying to get her first book published but she had very little time to write any of it. She was a full time worker, a full time single mom of 5 children and she had no family to look after the kids for a little while so that she could work on her writing, let alone finding the right publisher. All she had time to do was write for about 20 minutes in the subway on her way home and on her way to work. She used that time as efficiently and as effectively as she could, maximizing every moment she got. She also only had a grade 7 education so her spelling was not where it needed to be. As she prayed, God brought her a friend of a friend who served as editor of a magazine and offered to read over and edit her work for her.

- A young man struggled with his weight all his life. He was naturally a bit pudgier and he didn't have the money to go to the gym. He was also working full time to get his engineering degree and determined that the only time he had to work out would be on his own (not in a gym) and in the mornings for only 15 minutes. He realized that this would not be enough so he also researched some ways to incorporate healthy eating into his day. His office was full of people who brought in candy, pizza, pastas and sweets each day so he had to navigate carefully around that.

- Carly was a woman who had a very sick father who was unable to work. Her mother was also very sick so there was no income coming into the home. Carly either had to find time to go to work over and above her school time or the family was going to lose their home. Carly prayed for help because she was still quite young and unsure what to do. She felt guided to speak to her teachers and ask if an arrangement could be made for her to do her classes and her school work and also go to work to make money for the family. Knowing the context, the school allowed her to complete much of her work on her own time, before and after her demanding work schedule. Today, Carly has a great work ethic because she is grateful for the opportunities afforded to her.

- Fred got pink slipped and so he had lost his job. He wanted to start a cleaning business but had no capital. He had no family to turn to for help and his wife had just left him. He had to figure out how he was going to do all the things he needed to do, now that he was being faced with new realities. As he prayed for help, slowly all the pieces to help Fred started coming together: people from church offered to help him with aspects of his business, local community members offered to supervise his kids while he worked, and because he chose to offer significant discounts on his services to the members of the community, he didn't even need to advertise - news of his services were spreading rapidly.

- Malcolm had a family to take of and a job to go to but he was seriously struggling with an addiction to alcohol. Each night after work, he would find himself drawn to the local bar and would spend his pay cheque (and more) on drinks. His family was waiting for him to put food on the table and his wife was physically disabled so they were mainly relying on him. Night after night, Malcolm would go to the pub and spend spend spend. He then developed an addiction to gambling in an effort to try to make some money for his family's needs. Everything was spiraling for him and he felt crushed by the weight of the world. His wife began praying for him to find his way and to stop destroying their family. She asked him many times to go to AA meetings so that he could get the help he so badly needed. For months, Malcolm refused, insisting he could handle the problem on his own but night after night he would drink away and then gamble away more than they even had. When his wife informed him that they were two months behind on rent and they would lose the residence, Malcolm relented and went to a meeting, as long as his wife attended with him. They managed to get her sister to babysit the kids and Malcolm began to face his issues in the AA meetings. Several years later, many AA meetings later and marriage counseling under their belt, today Malcolm and his family are thriving - their marriage stronger, Christ-based and filled with hope, their children thriving at school and getting ready for college and Malcolm having started being present in the lives of his family and not drinking away the family funds.

- Rich became a church leader. He began to lead the local church's Bible study sessions but began becoming puffed up with pride. He began to see the trust that parishioners had started putting in him in asking for his help in managing their lives and their faith journeys but he turned away and let people know that he was not available to help. People began to see that he was unwilling to help. Cheryl did not know where else to turn as she was new to the area and did not know any of the other church leaders. She knocked on Rich's door several times for help, for some guidance, for any assistance. You see, Cheryl had discovered her husband had been cheating on her and that he refused to stop. She was completely confused about what to do as they had 3 children together and she was feeling very scared, not wanting to break her marriage vows and walk away from her husband. Cheryl prayed for what to do. She felt the Holy Spirit guiding her to pray deeply for her husband and to not approach Rich about the issues any longer. Cheryl was in need of help, not to be there to help a church leader who had become puffed up. Cheryl prayed relentlessly for her husband for 2 years before he finally relented and agreed to go to counseling together. In counseling, her husband opened up about his inadequacies as a husband and how he felt there was no way Cheryl could love a loser like he felt he was, so he went to seek comfort in the arms of another. Cheryl worked an extra job to be able to pay for the counseling sessions since her husband had, at that point, fallen into a deep depression and was unable to go to work anymore and they had lost their health insurance. For two and a half years, Cheryl and her husband attended counseling, dove into their issues and their feelings of inadequacy toward each other and discovered that despite everything, they were still very much in love and that they actually both wanted the marriage to work. Cheryl had to persevere through rejection and humiliation to get to the other side - success and happiness with her husband.

- Ramin was a med student and he knew his resident doctor did not see a leader in him. He knew that he needed to work extra hard to get his resident doctor to select him for the leadership roles he desired but for some reason, the resident doctor had it out for him. He would be blatantly unfair to him, treating him in a diminutive capacity and causing him to be passed up for opportunities. Ramin worked very hard, came in early and left late each day. He did not know what else to do. This resident doctor was the only one who could promote him in the hospital. He began praying for insight on how to handle things and he felt that he was being guided to stay the course at that hospital. For years, Ramin continued to be passed up. He continued to be the least selected, even though he was putting in more work than the others. Ramin kept doing what he needed to do, trying his best not to complain, trying his best to focus on the work and not on his mistreatment. Finally, an opportunity Ramin would have been perfect for presented itself and again, he was not considered. Another supervisor asked him if he even wanted to be a doctor because he kept getting passed up. Ramin explained that he certainly wanted to be a doctor but that he kept getting passed up for opportunities by the resident doctor. The other supervisor said that he had a position for him but that would have required him moving out of the area he was familiar with and to move to a new area that he was completely unfamiliar with. Ramin prayed over it and he decided that he was being given a great opportunity and so he took it. His rise from that point was extremely fast and even though it was in an area he had never planned to practice, he realized that it was a blessing and so he shifted those gears.

Life does not always present us with fair situations. You may get passed up unfairly for promotions, you may get put down or not be supported by your superiors or your peers, you may be outright mocked. The art of getting it done and being an overachiever who gets it done means that you persevere past those hurts and those pains and you will come out better and the victor on the other side.

Not Supposed To Do It Alone

One of the most important things I would like to state in more than one way in this book is that we are not supposed to do any of this alone. On our own.

Yes, we are supposed to work hard (God is not going to do that for us) but we are supposed to rely on Him for His strength and His help.

A lady I was talking to at one time (I will name her Charisma) said that she enrolled in a Masters course and that she was feeling very overwhelmed. She felt that she had a decent grasp on the material but that her professor had said that that was not enough. She had indicated to me that she had a bit of experience with the subject matter but not enough of a grasp on it and was not even able to understand the professor's new teachings. I asked her if she had asked God for help. She said that she had not and that she had never even thought of asking Him for His help.

Friend, ask Him. He wants to be asked, whatever situation you find yourself in, He wants to be asked and He wants that relationship with you. Yes, relationship - because it is a loving, kind and the best relationship you can ask for.

A week later I followed up with her and asked her if she had prayed for help and to see how things were going. She shared that she had prayed for some help, any help, and shortly thereafter received an email from her professor advising of online extra help sessions that were available to all students at no additional charge as well as the opportunity to meet with him one on one online and to get help for any questions they may have. She talked about how she had attended one of the sessions and that she learned so much in that one session that she felt propelled to complete all her work for that course section and that she felt very confident (for the first time) in her responses. She also explained how she felt so much better about her own abilities and that she had stopped feeling "stupid", were her words.

You see, friend, the Lord is there and remains at the ready to help. You need to ask for it and you also need to keep in mind that the way that the Lord may help you may not be the way you think He is going to help you. He is going to help you in the way(s) that He knows is the best for you, not necessarily in the way you think is best.

For example, when I was speaking to Charisma, she thought that the only way she would receive help would be by asking her professor to guide her to reading resources online where she would be able to read up and learn a bit more about how something needed to be done. She never dreamed that the professor would actually hold free extra help sessions online because others had told her that the professor was not very courteous with his time, so she didn't bother asking for that. When I advised her to pray, I advised her to pray in general and to leave the means up to the Lord. She did that and received more than she thought she would.

One more example here is the example of Johnny. Johnny came from a very broken home and he had been bounced back and forth in foster care. He was deeply unhappy and felt ready to give up on life. He had also met Marie and they had had an unplanned pregnancy. Johnny felt like things could not get worse but during one of his classes, his teachers had advised him to pray to Jesus when he felt overwhelmed and that he had no way out. So, Johnny prayed. He asked the Lord to come into his life and to help him because he didn't know where to turn or how to "do life" anymore. Slowly but surely, things began to change for Johnny. He was adopted by a Pastor and his wife who were having trouble conceiving on their own, and moved into their home where he learned more about prayer. The Pastor taught him how to use his hands and Johnny learned the trade of being a carpenter. He began picking up jobs here and there and began to see that not only was he good at being a carpenter, but that he actually enjoyed it (and he was starting to make good money from it). He still felt unsure about the new baby that was coming and prayed to God about what to do. Help arrived quickly. The Pastor's wife asked him about what else was going on in his life and Johnny opened up about the unplanned baby. The Pastor's wife began to explain to Johnny that even though the pregnancy was unplanned, that it didn't mean the baby was a mistake. She advised him on how to treat Marie like a lady and they resolved that they were going to do all that they could to provide a good and happy life for the baby. Today (as of this book's writing), Johnny and Marie are married, attend online church regularly, Johnny makes a very good living as a carpenter, their son Teddy is thriving at school and Marie decided to use the times that Teddy was away at school to educate herself and become a paralegal. Johnny to this day credits the love of God for what He has done for him in his life.

When we ask God for help, we are doing something very wise. He has ways that we don't, strategies we often don't think of on our own and He has ways to open doors that no man can shut.

Will things sometimes be inconvenient? Yes. But inconvenient is not a bad thing and when something good is inconvenient but we do it anyway, we have a tremendous sense of satisfaction that is truly awesome. When something is very difficult but we persevere, the sense of accomplishment afterward is truly amazing and we feel very empowered.

Chapter 12

Learning Something New

Oftentimes, when it comes to being an overachiever, it means that we will have to pick up a new skill or that we will have to refine a skill we already have but we don't know very well.

Many overachievers and people who have mastered the art of getting it done know that we cannot always rely on others - we sometimes need to do things ourselves in order to complete them within the time frame and in the way that are needed. Oftentimes, one step relies on a previous step and we cannot always rely on others to accomplish that step for us, in the way and within the time frame that we will need. Put differently, if we are always waiting on others, we will be wasting valuable time because really simply, many people are not or will not be as motivated as us to create your dream and to work at building your dream. They will not be willing to wake up at 4 am and work on the task that is needed, they will not be willing to cut short or take time out of their vacation to work on something that requires immediacy, they won't be willing to work for the wages that you can offer, and so on and so forth.

Oftentimes, we have to get used to doing things ourselves. And that often means that we will have to pick up a new skill and do something that we didn't think we were going to have to delve into.

In addition, new technologies, new designs and new processes are and will continue to crop up. We have to stay abreast of these changes because they are the evolving of society and we have to make sure that we are staying on top of new and better ways (often cost-cutting ways too) of doing things.

When you are an overachiever, you make it your business to stay on top of the new updates and the new ways. Your employees will likely not because you haven't paid them to do so. It's your dream - you're going to have to work at it and diligently so.

Sure, there will be times when we need staff to complete work (I am not discrediting that) but when times get tough or you need to buckle down and get something done within a tight time frame, for example, your employee will not work for you the way that you work for you. This is why many times I believe some of the most successful businesses are family-owned and family-run businesses - you are more likely to trust your family than you are to trust regular (non family) employees or hires.

Refine That Skill

Sometimes, we already have the basics of the new skill down pat, but we need to further our skills. This is also very important because it is sometimes not enough to just know or understand the basics of something. I needed to learn how to create websites because I knew that my website would require relatively frequent updating, would require new technologies to be updated, and much more. I tell you that I had hired someone to do much of the work for me in the early days when I didn't have a great handle on setting up websites but the person did not always follow through or didn't follow through in the way that I had instructed, didn't want to do the job within the time frame that was needed, and when I would bring this up to the person I had hired, he simply said that he hadn't had time to do it.

People will not care about your dream the way you do. They are likely going off and working on building their own dream. So, this means that if you want something done and done right and done within the time frame you are looking for, then realize and accept that you will likely need to learn to do it yourself.

This does not have to be an overwhelming concept. Not at all. Learning something new can be great fun, exciting, and people generally feel a great sense of satisfaction and worthiness when they accomplish something that needed to be done. They tend to feel good because they know they have conquered the problem and have achieved something great.

I recall a lady with whom I was speaking and will call Gloria. Gloria felt called to be a graphic designer and wanted to work full time at this. The problem was that she had had zero training on how to be a graphic designer and felt that no company would hire her without the formal schooling. She also didn't have the funds to put herself through school in order to learn the craft. So Gloria did as she always did. She prayed. She prayed and asked Jesus how she was supposed to do this work that she did not have the proper training for. She prayed through the problem and she prayed through any and all feelings of inadequacy she felt as a result of not having had the proper, formal training. She shared that she felt led to self-educate by reading up on tools, strategies and techniques, by watching instructional videos, by watching others and seeing how they did things. See, another one of the great things about proverbially getting your hands wet and doing the work yourself is that you are able to see the intricate details of how something is supposed to be done, you are able to see why things are being done the way that they are and then, you can decide for yourself if that is the best way to continue doing something.

I discovered, as I was learning the skill of building websites, that many of the websites I was seeing were not built as well as they maybe could have been, especially when it came to the e-commerce portions. Had I not learned the trade myself and taught myself, I would never have been able to really see and understand the back-end of things, understood the way things worked and were connected to the payment systems, or used any of my learning to my advantage to make my website and presentation work more effectively and more efficiently, as well as to see what other, new features I can add to make my value offering even greater.

If I had just relied on a web person to continue building and adding to my site, there is no guarantee that that person would have pointed those things out to me or that I would have been educated enough to ask the right questions about how things work. Further, when we want to improve on processes, we need to understand how things work in order to make those improvements. Relying on others to do all the work for you in some ways limits your effectiveness because some employees are looking to finish their work time and go about their own business and their own lives.

You have to rely on yourself and the Holy Spirit to reach the levels you are being called to reach. You have to rely on yourself and the Holy Spirit to open your eyes to the new possibilities that exist to propel you and your endeavors further. Does it mean that the Holy Spirit will always guide you to do everything on your own? No, it doesn't. You have to pay attention to the guidance that is meant for you.

I believe many employees out there are phenomenal. They make businesses work, they provide great value offerings and many regularly go above-and-beyond as often as they can. But overachievers know that the dreams God has put on your heart will be achieved by you and by the Holy Spirit and they may involve employees, or they may not.

Another example that comes to mind is the work a lady I used to know also named Christine was engaged in. Her family had started a catering business and they were very successful. We had met in teacher's college and she would regularly talk to us about the orders she needed to fill, how she was going to make the orders after securing the necessary wholesale supplies and how she often needed to work hard and work overtime to deliver the goods to the job site because her "regular delivery person" was unable to for one reason or another. She had a regular delivery person but when they were unable to fulfill their duties for one reason or another, Christine could not simply leave the order (and the food already made) spoil.

She therefore had to find a way to get the goods safely into her little car and she made the route over to the job site even when it was terribly inconvenient. I recall how many fun activities, family get-togethers, time with her husband and kids she had to give up in order to get the order filled. She had to rely on herself and the resources at her disposal in order to get things accomplished.

Learning A New Language And New Ways

In previous books, I have spoken about my great aunt, Nada, who came to Canada without much and not speaking any English. She came to Canada searching for a better life and better opportunities. She did not have much in terms of education and she spoke no English but she felt incredibly led by God to come and to make a new life for herself here (this book was also written in Canada). So what did Nada do? She got to work. She began attending free English as a Second Language classes at the local library, she began listening to English music and stories on tape, she began learning about how the school system works in Canada and enrolled herself in school to become an engineer. She knew she needed money to support herself so she worked part time as a cashier, a job she figured would not require her to speak too much because she still had a very heavy foreign accent. What was Nada doing? She was working hard to improve her life and to do what needed to be done for that better life. She learned new skills, and buckled down to really get to work. She learned English in less than a year because before school and work each morning, she would review her English notes and she would make sure that she always checked-in with her teachers to make sure that she was on the right track.

After all, nobody said being an overachiever was going to be easy.

Chapter 13

BIG Goals

Like all of the examples given, all the people had big goals and big dreams. And they were willing to work hard to achieve them.

When we have big goals and big dreams, there are a number of things we can do to make those big goals and big dreams easier and more palatable to achieve. In other words, how can we make these sometimes-seemingly massive tasks just a bit easier and more manageable? Simple. Start with all of the following six helpful tools:

1. A Well Defined Goal - having well-defined goals is of vital importance. If we don't know what we are aiming for, we are sure that we will not hit that.
2. Strategic Steps - if we are not strategic in our steps, again, we will be sure to not hit the goal. Strategic steps simply means that we are not just taking action, but instead, we are taking Holy Spirit-inspired actions that you have prayed over.

3. Strategy Mind Maps - this can and will look differently for many. Strategy mind maps are simply the road map you see yourself taking that will lead to the convictions, thoughts, actions, and more that you see happening in an effort to lead to where you need to be. A mind map is how you visualize it in your mind. Again, you don't need to come up with this yourself - let the Holy Spirit guide you on this.
4. Pay Attention to Opportunities that present themselves - where the Lord leads you, He will provide for you. As such, we do not have to worry about how we will get something (or all things) done. He will show us the way and we would be wise to keep our eyes peeled for doors that suddenly open. Now, I want to impress upon you to pray over the doors that open or seemingly open. What I mean by this is that doors may open but you would be wise to pray to make sure that it's the right door that God is opening. Other doors can also open and with the intent to mislead you and misguide you. You have to be wary and cautious of this.
5. Asking God To Step In - you and I and everybody else were never meant to do everything on our own. God is supposed to be helping you through it, which means that when He guides you to something and you find it very difficult, ask Him to step in, ask Him to make happen what you cannot make happen on your own. God is supposed to be your Partner but if you don't engage Him, He will not be. Engaging Him can be as simple as praying "God, I don't know what I'm supposed to do here, help me understand" or "This door is not opening for me...what should I do?" He will answer you every time (not necessarily right when you want Him to, but He will answer and help).

6. Accepting Help From Certain Others - when you receive help from people, such as family members, friends, or others, pray over whether it would be wise to accept help from them. Why? Because wolves can appear in sheep's clothing. In other words, you may think this person is there to help you but until you pray over their intentions, you will not know.

Referring to point #6, I will provide an example of help that is from God and help that isn't:

Help from God: A woman was struggling to start her business. She felt that she had received a wonderful idea for a business from God and she was starting to put the pieces together. As time went on, things were starting to smooth themselves out and the phone was beginning to ring with new work opportunities. She had been struggling to find the right person to help her with sales, so she prayed about it and felt led to approach a certain man. When she decided to follow up on that lead, she did approach that man, who kindly went out of his way to introduce her to some of his business colleagues and friends who were experts in the area. In return, he asked for only her friendship.

"Help" not from God: A woman was struggling with her co-workers who were being mean, nasty and it seemed like they were setting her up for a fair amount of failure. They were essentially trying to throw her under the bus. Seeing as she was new to the company, she decided to approach the company and division manager for help. She also conveyed to the manager that she was looking to be promoted, after proving herself within the company. She had worked there for a little while and the manager had gotten to know her and her work ethic (which was very strong). The manager offered some support and advised this woman that she had been doing a wonderful job. She had said that there was nothing wrong with her performance and to carry on. She had said that she would also speak to the parties involved and help to calm things down. As time progressed, things with her co-workers only got worse - a lot worse. She was openly mocked, her shared ideas were never taken and she was made to feel horrible each and every day. This went on for 5 months. Finally, she approached the manager again and said that things had gotten worse and she was looking for some help and some advice. The manager then called this woman into her office and berated her outright for her lack of work ethic, lack of being able to stand up for herself and for not lashing back out at her co-workers. She was being berated and chastised for not going down to the level of her unprofessional coworkers and instead, doing her work. The manager made it seem as though she had her support. Nothing could have been further.

Breaking Goals Down

Like with many other things that seem grand and can feel overwhelming, breaking down our goals into manageable steps and processes is a wonderful tool. Most things that are grand in acquisition will require consistent work and consistent effort, something that needs to be worked on. A large goal is no different. So, break down that goal into manageable steps and write down your steps on a piece of paper or on a device. This will make it much more manageable in your mind's eye and you will be able to see how that big goal is not so overwhelming anymore.

Don't Share Your Ideas With Everyone

When you have an idea that God has put on your heart, here is a suggestion: don't share it with others. People (even those who are well-meaning) can let the air out of your proverbial tires and can discourage you from taking on a big goal. They don't know your drive, they don't know your sense of Spirit, they don't know what and why God has put this on your heart and they may be speaking as just ones who feel that they would never be able to undertake those goals.

No need to share your ideas.

The best thing to do when God puts an idea on your heart is to spend some time letting it marinate in your mind and in your heart. Opening your Bible or Bible app would also be tremendous because that is one of the main ways that the Holy Spirit speaks to us. Pray over the situation and your first steps with that Bible open and see what senses, feelings, inklings, etc., you get.

It is important to note that even people who mean well in your life and who are generally pretty supportive of you may still let the air out of your tires with your idea. They may be rushed, preoccupied, they may not be listening carefully to what you're saying, they may not be ones who pray themselves or who have any relationship with God and therefore wouldn't know that you are being led and supported by God in this endeavor.

So do yourself a favor and don't reveal your idea or the details thereof until you get clear indication from God that it is time to share with select people.

Those With Whom To Share

I want to be very clear here in saying that the ones with whom you should eventually share (when God gives you the green light to do so) are with those who will be very supportive. I will qualify what very supportive means. A person being very supportive means that they will reinforce what and how God has told you to proceed. Being a very supportive person also means that they are a person who will help provide you with solid help and advice. For example, a person being very supportive means that they know a lot about the particular industry or context which you are looking to make your foray into and can give you helpful tips and pointers about everything to do with that.

I remember when I was applying to teacher's college and I didn't know much about the industry or how to proceed, I had a few helpful people who were telling me how to navigate the particular teacher's college I wanted to attend, explaining the course work and about the professors and talking to me about US to Canada course and program equivalencies. Bear in mind that I only went out to seek the help once I felt sure that the time was right to share the info and my future career path.

A Last Word

A last word about big goals: do not feel overwhelmed by them. Yes, it can seem a bit overwhelming at first, especially because God does not usually give goals that are commensurate with our bank accounts - He doesn't look only at our bank accounts and what is currently there because He owns everything and He can bring us all the resources we need at any time. Instead, step out and take the first step He provides in faith.

Chapter 14

Helpful Angels

I believe we all know and have experienced people who wish us unwell and those who do us unwell. People who do not want good things to happen for us and who either will outright try to sabotage or who are more subtle in their level of un-support (yes, I created a new word).

But what about those who are helpful angels? Those who do go out of their way to help us?

Those people also exist and while they may be few and far between, they are there and we should celebrate them.

Helpful angels refers to any people, pets or things who want the best for you and let you know either outright or subtly that they are supporting you. These people can be anyone from a parent who supports you, friends, co-workers and colleagues, an acquaintance, a pet or even a book or a resource.

Helpful angels are those who provide some help for you in the ways that you require it, doing anything from the list below or beyond:

- Emotional support
- Making you a meal
- Spending time with you on the phone to help you feel better
- Praying with you
- Texting you
- A pet who provides support
- Talking through a problem with you
- Guiding you to a passage of Scripture that directly relates to your situation
- A person inviting you to a Bible-based Church (either face to face or online) where you can get Spiritual nourishment
- Physically supporting you by perhaps, helping you work out or helping you do yoga
- Providing you with some seed money for your endeavor
- Picking up your kids from school on days when you cannot
- Talking to your kids about important topics
- Being a helpful taste-tester or someone who samples your products or services with the intention to help support you
- A person who helps you practice your presentation & gives constructive feedback
- A person who reminds you to breathe through a hard time
- A person who lovingly supports you to losing weight and becoming more fit
- A person who lets you stay with them until you get your bearings together

You see, readers, support can come from anywhere and from anyone. Helpful angels are any people or living beings (I am including pets in this) who lend you the support that you need. And we all need that support. No matter what you are trying to achieve, there are going to be some challenges attached to it. That is part of any goal. But helpful angels are those people who work hard to be there and to support you when you need it. It can be texting you at 2 am to help you not eat the cookie dough, or it can be a person who stays up with you to help you complete that project you have been working so hard on. Either way, we all need helpful angels.

Tech Can Be Very Handy Here

When we are working hard on something, it may mean that we cannot physically be with our helpful angels. Technology helps a lot in this case. With apps, our smartphones and the use of tech, we can connect with people in ways not seen before. We can connect and have people help us (and we can help them) when we cannot physically be in the same space.

If you are one of those people who is a little uncertain about how to use tech to connect with people, there are many library programs, and services that can help you learn how to use these new techy gadgets. I completely understand how it may feel for people who are new to this and who may be feeling overwhelmed, but we have to persevere and step by step, see how we can use these tools to our advantage. Please consider this as your invitation to dive into the world of tech and to begin to help yourself to learn how to use these to your advantage.

"What If I Don't Have Anyone, Christine?"

There are many people who do not have people to help them. They may not have friends or family around them to help them learn, to help support them and they may be feeling quite alone. The best thing to do is to pray. Pray for God to bring you at least one person who will be able to help you, to be there for you and to act as a kind touchstone.

When we are in any kind of lack, the smartest and best thing we can do is to go to God with our problem and to ask Him for His help. We always want to ensure that we go to Him with our problems because He loves us and cares for us more than anyone.

When you pray for help, will it always necessarily come immediately? Sometimes not. But bear in mind that God is always listening and be comforted by the fact that if it hasn't come yet, it is because God is working on it on your behalf. It is not because He has refused you.

If you have prayed for companionship of any kind, listen carefully to the Holy Spirit inside - He may be encouraging you to attend a meeting you recently heard about, He may be encouraging you to reach out to a specific person, etc. Be assured that that is God's way of answering your prayer. That is His way of bringing to your mind the answer to your prayer. In other words, the person, community or individuals He brings to your mind is His answer that they are the ones He is guiding you to connect with because it will likely go well with them.

Chapter 15

Managing Disappointment

I want to make it clear here that managing disappointment is a big part of the process of becoming an overachiever. Obstacles come to everyone and we will sometimes get and feel disappointment in the process of accomplishing what we are looking to accomplish.

This is not a bad thing.

I often regard disappointment as God's way of letting us know that this is not going to come easily and without effort but that it is going to be worth it in the end.

> When things come to us (too) easily, we do not value them as much. When we have to work hard or really hard to accomplish something, we value that thing so much more and the ensuing sense of satisfaction from the accomplishment is just fantastic!

Think of the last time something did not come easily to you and that you had to work really hard to figure out a way to make sure you accomplished it. I will bet that if you did see it through, that you may likely now feel a tremendous sense of accomplishment with it and that you may be feeling really good that you managed to get it done, despite all the obstacles.

Biblically, God did not always make it easy for ordinary people to accomplish extraordinary things. He did not make it easy for Abraham to have his son, He did not make it easy for Mary to conceive and give birth to Jesus, He did not make it easy for Moses to cross the Red Sea. In turn, Jesus did not have it easy when He had to fast for 40 days and 40 nights and then be tempted by satan afterward and not fall into his prey. Nobody has it easy and as such, each person's story is that much more meaningful, that much more special and that much more noteworthy.

Think of how noteworthy it will be when you accomplish step 1, 2, 3, 4 and so on of your goals. Think about how you will feel. Think about how awesome you will feel having had that sense of accomplishment.

Personally, I don't always like to focus on the accolades and compliments of others. It isn't my favorite thing to do because people can just tell you what you want to hear and it isn't necessarily the truth. Instead, I like to focus on the pillars and benchmarks that I have set for myself. For example, when my friend Becca realized that she was overweight in an unhealthy way, she decided to set pillars and benchmarks for herself at each stage, deciding to celebrate with a bit of fat-free frozen yogurt when she reached a weight loss of 5 lbs, 10 lbs, 15 lbs and so on.

She was making great strides in this and when people encouraged her to "just have that piece of cake, you're already doing great" she wisely chose not to listen. She chose to ignore the comments and encouragement to eat the piece of cake because while it would have possibly felt gratifying in that moment, it would have completely derailed her weight loss efforts and accomplishments thus far.

When you have a disappointment in your path, lament it for a moment but then, get back on the proverbial horse. Don't allow yourself to stay down.

When you have a disappointment in your path, understand what went wrong and what happened, and choose to move forward and move past it in a productive way.

When you have a disappointment in your path, try not to get disappointed by the setback and instead, focus on moving forward more positively and in a more mindful way.

Lastly, when you have a disappointment in your path, acknowledge that you are human and that you will make mistakes and write down how you are going to commit to ensuring that it doesn't happen again.

These strategies can be applied to just about any challenging endeavor you take on, from trying to get promoted, to trying to lose weight, to working hard at being a better wife or parent, to endeavoring to get into that school or that program that is really meaningful to you, to endeavoring to get pregnant and the list goes on and on.

> You can get discouraged but don't allow the setback keep you down.

Keep in mind that one day, you will look back on the process and you will realize that the setback was temporary and that you didn't allow it to keep you down. No, instead, you got back up, you proverbially dusted yourself off and you chose to keep going on your path to betterment and you chose to see past that temporary disappointment.

The fact is, if you allow that disappointment to keep you down and you do not continue on your path to working hard at your goal, what you are basically doing is subconsciously allowing that temporary disappointment to keep you down and to continue to make you feel bad. This is the worst possible thing for any person. Why? Because if you get back on the horse after say, 1 day of feeling down instead of getting back on the horse after say, 15 days of feeling down, you will have had 14 days more to work hard at your goal and realistically, you will be much further ahead as a result of getting back up sooner.

Readers, this is why I say that focus and discipline are so important. They both teach us that we are to hold ourselves accountable for our actions and those actions begin with empowering thoughts.

Empowering Thoughts

When we wish to engage in empowering actions, those empowering actions begin with empowering thoughts. Empowering thoughts are those thoughts that serve you well and that take you a long way in committing to your goals. Empowering thoughts are those thoughts that remind you that you are a warrior and that you are doing a great job, despite those pesky obstacles. Empowering thoughts are those that remind you to stay on route despite what other people are saying.

Remember, people may sometimes have our best interests at heart but their approach is not always helpful. We have to access the Holy Spirit to determine if the comment we just heard is really one that is in our best interest or if it is one that is going to derail us.

As an example, I encountered a woman I will call Jana who was working really hard to get into law school. She had poured over the books, she had studied really hard but was still not managing to pass the exam to get to the next step. She had failed a couple of times and was now getting more and more frustrated. Those around her who were not necessarily onboard with her achieving her endeavor kept asking her if this much work was really worth it. They kept telling her that this goal was too hard for her and that she should set her sights on alternative goals. She chose not to listen. She really felt she was being guided by God to be a civil lawyer. Instead, she decided to really buckle down. She studied harder than she ever had before, asked her professors for extra help, joined study groups and purchased practice exams. She studied extremely hard for the next upcoming exam and sure enough, it was the closest she had ever gotten to passing. On the very next try, after even more studying and even more effort, she passed the exam with flying colors.

What can we take from Jana's example?

It won't be easy. It's not supposed to be. But it will be worth it if you stick to it and the feeling of accomplishment and satisfaction will be well worth it. Today, Jana is a very successful lawyer and those who encouraged her to give up continue to do the exact same things with others that they did to Jana - disempowering people from God's plan for them.

A last point I'd like to make about disempowering people: many times, we will have friends and family around us who give us their opinions on what they think we should do. This is not always the wisest course of action.

Please take the question to God. Let Him speak to you through the Holy Spirit.

> Please take the question to God. Let Him speak to you through the Holy Spirit.

This means that you are to let God guide your actions in how to do something, the right timing, the right pacing once you are in it and so on. People have not called you to do that thing and people are not God. God is the One who called you to do it and God is the One who will be there to help you and guide you in His perfect ways.

Get Out Of There If You Need To

At times, we can find ourselves in situations where people are really unsupportive and are actively trying to deter us from doing what we are supposed to do on our path to our goals. In this case, it could be best to remove yourself from the situation. Be mindful that we are only human and we are susceptible to the suggestions of others. So, when that aunt or that cousin tells you that "you've done enough, now you can relax" or "don't bother with it, it's too much", those comments are sometimes not designed to help you. Those comments are subconsciously or consciously intended to derail you.

Going back to the example of Jana just above, those people were not trying to be helpful but they were trying to tear Jana down. Engaging in the conversation is engaging in the battle and it is not necessary and we don't have to do it. Getting out of there and spending your time with empowering people would be much better for you!

Be mindful and wary of those who are trying to sway you in one way or another. Take the question to God before you take it to anyone else. Enjoy the empowering, loving, supportive conversation with God because He is the One who will not only tell you the truth about where you really are but He will also guide you to the people who will actually empower you.

Chapter 16

Managing Stress & The Inconvenient - The Drive To Succeed

When we feel uncertain and we feel like we are not sure of what is going to happen, stress occurs. Virtually everyone experiences it at some point and it is something we have to manage.

Stress comes from not knowing where your strength comes from. We can sometimes forget our own abilities and capacities and that can make us consciously or subconsciously question ourselves.

> We are never called to do things on our own - we are called to do things with God.

This is where we have to stop and remind ourselves that we have what it takes to get through this difficult situation. We are never called to do things on our own - we are called to do things with God. He is there to help us, to guide us, to talk to us through the uncertainties and the worries and above all, to see us through something.

He will never guide us to something that He is not able to bring us out of. That's the simple fact. In other words, if He has guided you to it, He will bring you through it. One of the smartest things to do when you are experiencing those moments of worry, stress and indecision is to pray about it and ask the Holy Spirit to help you through it.

When James was worried about proposing to his girlfriend, he knew he needed to consult with God to get His help. He felt deeply in his sense of self that this was something God was calling him to do but he felt worried. When he asked the Holy Spirit for help, the Holy Spirit helped him see that this was not so much about a proposal, but more so about a conversation about the future with this woman and how he needed to be more comfortable having deeply personal and in-depth conversations with her. That's a big part of what marriage is.

When Naomi was looking to register for the hockey team but she knew she was not yet on-par skillswise with those she could see trying out in front of her, she prayed about it and knew that it was a matter of working on her game and refining her skills and that that would make her much more confident and comfortable in trying out for the team. Accordingly, she spent months working on her game and alas, she was definitely put on the team.

When Jeremy was applying to dental school but he wasn't getting the responses he was looking for because he knew that he hadn't done his best in his first year of university which was dragging down his whole average, he felt stressed and prayed about how to handle it. The Holy Spirit guided him to the right school which was further from home but ultimately, would accept his lower grades and put him on a brief probationary period to give him an opportunity to show them what he was capable of. Was it inconvenient for him to go so much further away from home and to be away from everyone and all he knew just so that he could follow his dream? For Jeremy, yes, because he knew that this temporary situation was needed in order to fulfill what God was calling him to do. He knew that this was an opportunity for which God had opened the doors for him and he was not going to let it slip by him.

Charisse wanted very much and felt called to be her church's gospel singer. The challenges were that she had never taken any singing lessons, her family did not have the funds to pay for those and she was shy about approaching her church pastor to request that she be made a singer for the choir. Charisse was a young girl but she had watched her grandmother and her mother pray deeply for things they needed and had seen how God had provided. As such, Charisse prayed deeply that if it was God's will, that a way be opened for her. Within two weeks, Charisse was offered free singing lessons by the current choir leader and a guaranteed spot singing in the church choir at the completion of those lessons. Charisse loves to sing with the choir now and her skills have come a very long way.

William had always felt stupid. His teachers had told him that he would likely not be able to go to university because he was in the special education class at his school and wasn't excelling in that program either. The paperwork in William's file also showed aggressive behavior and he was regularly mouthing off to people around him. William was angry because he knew he wanted to go to university and be an engineer like his absent dad but felt powerless in trying to get there with every grade he got back being either a fail or a near-fail. William's mother prayed for him - for a way to be made for William to find his strength and his voice and sure enough, William's teacher had decided to implement a peer tutoring program. William's mom had a talk with him about how helpful this program could be and he decided to give it a try. The teacher placed him with a very kind young girl who was able and willing to take time to further explain things to William and to help him understand how to organize his work and how to write out his assignments and due dates. Over several months, William's work, grades and attitudes changed considerably. William shared how he was working hard and he began praying for God to open up more and more doors for him. Despite initially feeling stupid and inadequate, William realized that he needed to work hard at the opportunities God had placed in his path.

When Carissa had an important presentation to deliver at work but wasn't given the tools by her new boss to do so, she felt lost and scared. She was in a new job and wasn't sure how she was going to handle this. She wanted desperately to do a great job in her work but she wasn't sure how she was going to manage something like this without the proper training, something her new and very busy boss was unwilling to give her. Carissa's friend suggested she pray about the job and the presentation. Carissa's friend had sensed that this was not the right job for her to have taken but that's another great thing about God, even when He hasn't called you to something but you ask Him for help because you are in it, He will help you and see you through it. Carissa's friend had indicated that the job was not where Carissa was supposed to be but that God would help her figure out a way. Carissa's husband asked her what was going on and why she was so worried and stressed lately. She then shared about the presentation she had no training for and her husband helpfully chimed in with "I know a bit about that and I can show you." Over the next few days, her husband was able to help her learn and understand the model that she would need to present on and she began to feel less scared. She worked hard at learning and at preparing the presentation even though her boss and her work place were offering nothing in terms of help and training.

Abby loved acting. She felt she was called to be an actress on Broadway and loved everything about acting from the smell of the stage to the costumes. She didn't even mind the idea of being in the hair, makeup and costume chair for long periods of time, letting the artists there work on transforming her into a character that she needed to portray, different from her own. The problem was that Abby first of all got a real feel of the stage that caused her to stutter significantly and then she was also not in a position where she was provided with any speaking roles because she was a back-up and had not yet been given any lead opportunities. Abby's pastor suggested that she pray over the situation and for God to open the doors at the time that He knew was right for her. He also suggested getting a dialect coach to help her get more comfortable with her lines because preparation for your goals is key. It was very important for Abby to learn about presenting herself more confidently on stage and how to get more lost in the character she was playing. Abby knew that this was a direct response to her prayers and she began working with a dialect coach and praying for the right opportunity to come up so that when the time was right, she would go up on stage. A small part presented itself that did not allow Abby to be completely made up but to be more natural - something that scared her because in her training, she got into the frame of mind of getting lost in her character. The bottom line was that Abby had to do it a little bit afraid and that she would need to begin putting into practice the coaching she had received on being a more confident speaker. Her first role was a bit of an improvement from her earlier days but she knew she still had a ways to go and that's ok, she knew she was improving.

Readers, oftentimes, we expect and we want results immediately. Life doesn't always work out that way. We are not promised to get exactly what we want in the exact way that we want it. Nope. If we receive the blessing, it will be done in God's timing and in His ways (at least, that's what happens when you rely on Him).

When Jessica wanted to open her own financial services company, something she felt strongly led to do, she knew that she wanted to open it in her hometown of Vancouver, British Columbia. But God had other plans. Jessica had also prayed to meet the man she would marry and to have children with him. Well, she did meet him and he was from Ohio and for his work, he was unable to move to Vancouver to be with her. So, if Jessica really wanted this relationship (which she felt deeply was the right thing for her) to work, she would have to move to Ohio and set up her new practice there. She knew this was not going to be easy and she prayed for God to give her the strength to do this and for Him to line things up for her. It was not easy for Jessica to manage and navigate everything that was coming up in her life (yes, even blessings can be hard to manage) but things were coming together. She felt very afraid to open up a new financial services company in a new country and was unsure of the laws, etc. Her new beau guided her to start this online which would help reduce the start-up costs and would allow her a more global reach. He offered to help her with it with any time he was able to give up from his own work. Things were starting to come together beautifully for Jessica - not in the way she had thought but nevertheless.

When Mark was ready to start a family, he was as single as can be. He was not a man who enjoyed going to bars or clubs nor was he interested in meeting the right woman online. Mark was a very faith-driven man and he prayed to God that He would bring him the right woman. Instantly, Mark's former high school sweetheart, Alexa, came to mind. He felt God guiding him to her but hadn't spoken to her in years. When he finally discovered how and there she was, he found out that she had been in rehab for a dependency on alcohol. Mark was totally perplexed and wasn't sure how to handle this revelation. He wondered why God would bring to his mind a woman who had these issues. When Mark finally got in touch with Alexa, she explained that after their relationship, her new boyfriend had led her down a very abusive path and had encouraged her to abuse alcohol. Mark was perplexed because Alexa had never really been a big drinker during their relationship. Alexa confessed that initially, she began drinking as a way to numb the pain of the bad relationship, especially since she felt so heartbroken about how things had ended with Mark. That was news to him. He didn't know that the end of their relationship had hurt her so much or that she was next involved in an abusive one. Mark felt a great peace in his spirit at the thought of waiting for Alexa to heal in rehab and then to make another go of their relationship, armed with more years and greater sense of understanding of each other. He knew that Alexa was the person for him because he knew that despite her challenges, he would love her and want to support her through all of that. Mark's prayer was answered - just not in the way he thought it would be.

Being an overachiever who perseveres does not mean everything will come easily to you. Quite the opposite. It means that you have enough mindfulness and character to see something that is a blessing but that may not look the way you thought it was going to look. In all the examples provided in this chapter, we can see how each person struggled, prayed, and relied on God to open the doors. We also got to see that they had to wrap their minds around the fact that their blessing was not looking like anything they expected it to look like. They had to step up to the plate despite the challenges in front of them. They had to navigate the often choppy waters and really work at putting their faith in God and accessing their dreams, despite how it came to them.

Using Your Time Well

We all have many things to do. Each area of each of our lives requires time, care, attention and resources. Overachievers make sure that they are using their time as wisely as possible. This means that they are doing all they can to ensure that they are working as effectively and as efficiently as possible.

Let God Plan Your Day.

When God plans your day and when you are open to what He says, you are following the greatest possible path to the achievement of your goals. You are following His way of doing things and His way is the best way. Therefore, before you start your day, ask Him how you should plan out your day. Break it down in chunks if you would like and ask Him what should be done in the morning, afternoon, evening and so on.

There have been many times when I let Him plan my day out for me and was surprised by how much focus and time He guided me to take on one thing. For example, in writing this book, He guided me to take the entire day to write it, knowing that I had many other things I had to do in my day. Nevertheless, the instruction to work dutifully on this book was clear. I spent hours and hours and hours on it. When you decide to be obedient and become a writer like the Lord guides, you don't always see the full picture of what that will mean. You don't see the entire proverbial staircase. You just take the first step and then you see where you are supposed to go from there.

So, take the time and plan your day carefully. Do so with Him. Many people do a morning meditation before the craziness starts. That's the ideal time to ask how you should plan out your day. Remember to also ask follow up questions as you go (either in your mind or out loud) and ask what your day is supposed to look like.

Having The Faith To Allow Yourself To Be Guided

I will be the first to admit that it takes a significant amount of faith to allow oneself to be guided by God. By doing so, you are setting down your own "know-how" and you are acknowledging that He knows best. Saying in your mind something as simple as "God, guide me. Show me what I am supposed to do and how I am supposed to do this" is a powerful and courageous thing to do. It means you are letting go of the steering wheel and you are working diligently toward what He guides, not toward what you think is best.

It is a partnership and we are lucky and blessed to have it.

His Power, Your Situation

I believe my former professor, Dr. Patty Sadallah put it best: "When you engage God in your day, you are now working on your goals in partnership with Him, allowing His power and His abilities to be released into the situation."

We all know of difficult times and difficult situations where we have needed His help. Oftentimes, if He hadn't stepped in, things would not have gone well. Therefore, when you ask Him and engage Him, you are also releasing His power into the situation. You may be seeing that nothing is changing, nothing is improving and then all of a sudden, a total 180 degrees and everything has changed. That is the demonstrated power of God.

> Getting it done does not mean just leaving it all up to God. No. This is a partnership. You are supposed to be working together.

Now, to be clear, being an overachiever and getting it done and done right does not mean that you are leaving everything up to God. Nope. In a partnership, all parties are working toward the goal. This is no different. You are working toward the goal - the only thing is you don't know what the full picture of the completion of that goal will look like so that's where a healthy dose of faith comes in.

In the examples and case studies mentioned above, the people involved did not know how things were going to turn out. None of the individuals mentioned had any kind of "guarantee" that things were going to work out perfectly for them, or even really work out. We actually never really know if something is going to work out - that's part of life. But what we do know is that when we partner with God, we are putting the best chances for success in our corner and we are doing our best to follow His path in accomplishing something grand.

"Christine, I don't have that relationship with God"

This is one of the most common reasons I hear from people who have not yet entered or not yet experienced a close, loving bond with God and my first response is "yet!". You do not yet have that relationship with Him but it can be built.

Great relationships don't happen overnight. They take time, patience, understanding, support, and they take parties who are willing. If you have never even engaged God ever into your life or into your problems, take the first step today.

God will never, ever turn away from someone who goes to Him genuinely. How does He know you are genuine? Because He knows your heart. Even if you feel you have made tons of mistakes and you feel like you aren't even lovable anymore (or many people in the world have told you that you are not lovable or worth it), know now that God says that you are worth it and He is ready and willing to come into your life to help you with everything.

Chapter 17

Taking The Time, Doing It Right

It takes time to do something in the right way. It takes time to develop the ideas, map it all out, plan it properly and execute it with precision and with care. Creating a masterpiece takes time and it takes diligence.

A perfect example of this comes to mind: the tv show Frasier, starring Kelsey Grammer, David Hyde Pearce, the late John Mahoney, Jane Leeves, Peri Gilpin and more. The show aired on tv as a spinoff from the wildly successful, Cheers. Most people know that spin offs, if not done correctly, tend not to be very successful. Done correctly means all of the following:

- Characters that are very well defined and very well thought-out
- Plot that is clear and easy to understand
- Storylines that audiences can relate to

- An accurate characterization of the human experience
- Superb acting

One of the things that made the show Frasier so engaging is that it had all of these elements which are very clear to see when we watch the show. The sheer acting ability of the characters leaves us in awe. Kelsey Grammer talked about how important it was to cast superb players - people who were really gifted in their craft and who knew how to not just step into the role and lives of the characters, but who knew how to exemplify who that person was through all of the following techniques: dress, facial and body expressions, appearance, and really making the character their own. When we watch the show, we can see how gifted every actor selected is and was for their role. Kelsey talked about how painstaking the process of creating his characters was for him and the team creatively developing the plot, characters, storylines and more.

Creating a show that checks off so many of the items mentioned above is a process one has to navigate carefully because it is one that needs to respond to the human condition, be relatable, be interesting enough and one that makes the audience care about the characters. Why choose to do it as a spinoff of another show? Because it is often much easier to capitalize on the show or the character(s) that audiences already know and that audiences have come to embrace.

How does this relate to the art of getting it done? Simple. In any industry (and in this example I just happened to use the example of on of the most difficult things to create - an uber successful tv show), it is about careful planning, knowing your audience, working off of something that has worked before and developing characters and storylines that are going to grip your audience and not let go.

Creators

The creators of anything in this world that have seen uber success have done so because they have worked relentlessly worked hard, planned carefully and executed with passion and with purpose. They planned how something was going to be presented and done so in a way that is so superior because they took the time, factored many things in and really made sure they were being creative geniuses.

Another example of incredible success is that of Dr. Ben Carson - world-famous neurosurgeon. If you have seen the film, Gifted Hands, which is based on Carson's life, you can see the difficulties he went through and how diligent, consistent work got him to the point where he is now arguably the most gifted neurosurgeon in the world. In order to operate on the conjoined twins who were attached at the back of the head, Dr. Carson spent months researching how this could be done and preparing for it because it had never been done before.

Humans are creators. Made in the image of God, we are creators just like God is a creator. We can either create good things or we can create things that are going to be, ultimately, detrimental to society. I am a firm believer that when we stick to the unerring word of God, and we put into practice His values and teachings, we will be blessed and we will be blessing society as well.

Each person created in the womb of their mother has a special raison d'etre and a special destiny. When we discover what that is, and we begin to work toward that, we get to see the fullness of what God created in us.

We Are All Creators

As I said, we are all creators and when we take the time to work hard on something and we plan our time and our steps in tandem with God, we are creating beauty, we are developing and presenting the very best version of ourselves and when others see us doing this, we are helping to develop and create the very best versions of themselves too.

When others see us operating, they will almost inevitably be inspired. Inspiration can come from anywhere and anyone. So when you are developing yourself in a healthy way, you are working hard toward your goals and you are being the best version of yourself, the energy and the beautiful inspiration that comes from that is hard to miss.

Many people are often being guided by God but don't even know it. When you work diligently toward your passion, and that passion is in line with Scripture, you can feel good that you are taking the right steps toward your destiny.

Chapter 18

Self-Assuredness

Overachievers and people who get it done and done well are going to be fairly self-assured people. Yes, they can do things scared but they are doing it with a conviction, otherwise they wouldn't be doing it. Said differently, taking on important projects and goals is no easy feat and in order to work consistently at its realization, we work in a self-assured manner. If you do not, people will sense it from you and your leadership status will greatly diminish.

Now, I want to be careful here and say that being self-assured does not mean that you are a know-it-all and you believe that you and you alone have all the answers. No. It means that you have enough conviction of your own abilities in Christ and that you are able and willing to prove that to people who will not begin by giving you the benefit of the doubt.

We have all been in situations where we are challenged. People who will challenge what we say, what we do, even our most core beliefs. This is inevitable and it is your opportunity to show them that you have this confidence and that you are prepared for them to challenge you on it.

People who are self-assured demonstrate all of the following qualities and characteristics:

- They have confidence in themselves
- They have confidence in what they are saying and presenting
- They have and demonstrate conviction
- They are well-prepared and well-researched
- They know their playing field very well
- They know how to strategically navigate their playing field very well
- They do not allow themselves to be deterred by others who may not agree with them
- They do not shrink away from a debate discussion but they also know when to realize that they have made their point and that it's time to leave the debate
- If afraid, they are people who go up to bat even when they are afraid
- They know that if they don't speak up, things will not go their way and they work to avoid that undesirable reality

In the case of Depp vs. Heard, the American attorney represented Mr. Depp, Ms. Camille Vasquez was a relatively young and relatively inexperienced lawyer whom Depp chose to hire as his legal representation in the defamation suit. Ms. Vasquez and the legal team working with her understood and recognized what was at-stake here and that if they did not argue this case in a way that brought facts and evidence to the table, that the undesirable situation (in their eyes) of Ms. Heard winning the case was going to happen.

Therefore, this young team prepared well, they planned their timing, strategies and arguments and presented their case as so. Ms. Vasquez and her team got it done and done well by demonstrating and exemplifying all the qualities and traits that I described just above.

Conviction

In an effort to be self-assured, one should really also have conviction. Conviction is having a firmly held belief or opinion. If we do not have conviction, we will be lacking seriously in self-assuredness. And when the going gets tough (and it will) you need to rely on a healthy dose of conviction in order to make your points and successfully so.

Conviction also means choosing to stick to and defend one's values. Every time we work at something, we are demonstrating and defending where our values lie because it takes effort to work at demonstrating and defending our values. Our values necessarily are going to come through in everything that we do. I don't know and have not seen many people who argue convincingly for the other side very often.

Conviction is another way of saying your "why". Your reason for doing something has to be significant to you because this is what you are going to go back to when things get difficult and you begin questioning "why am I doing this?"

Chapter 19

Many Things

Some people hold the idea that they cannot do many things well or that one cannot be involved in many roles at the same time. I could not disagree more. I remember when I was growing up and I would tell people all the things I was involved in, every single person I spoke to told me that you cannot do so many things.

It is now years later and I know that that simply wasn't true.

We can do many things and we can do many things well. There are those who appreciate focusing on one thing and completing that before taking on something else, and that is fine. And then there are people like me who enjoy (even prefer) taking on many big projects at a time and while I have the same 24 hours as any other person, my way of dividing my time may be a bit different. I am not trying to say that I am better or that other people don't have the same abilities. No. I am only saying that there are those who enjoy taking on many large projects at once and they feel they are able to do them all at the same time. And that's great.

Allow yourself to be guided by the Holy Spirit and to do things in the way and in the order He guides.

A woman I know did all of the following things and she organized her time so that she could complete them all: real estate agent, dancer, videographer, mother, wife, sister, daughter, advertising executive and painter. When she had completed one task and was waiting for the next steps in that task, she went on to the next thing. For example, while she was cooking dinner for her kids, she would be texting with a client about a property, and then later emailing with her choreography director about how they were going to do the layout for the next dance and then put on her advertising exec hat and made an appointment with her team to discuss the new ad campaign for the following morning. She took it upon herself to do all of these things and she reported that while it wasn't easy, that each item was equally important to her soul. In addition to all of these things, she would be baking brownies for the church bake sale for which she had volunteered. Bravo to her!

Doing One Thing

Now, I believe it is also important to state here that if you are one of those people who feels led to be doing one thing at a time, then that is what is right for you. And there is nothing wrong with that. Again, we need to let God set the timelines and parameters for all we do.

We need to let God set the timelines and parameters for all we do.

The benefit of doing one thing and focusing on only that is that it affords us the luxury of really focusing on that one thing. Working on one thing (if that is how you work) is a way to ensure that you are really diving deep into that topic and considering it from all angles.

Again, you need to find your way - are you one who enjoys (or feels a necessity) in taking on one thing at a time or are you more so someone who enjoys taking on only one thing and working hard at that. Reflection time on this in a quiet space will definitely help you on that.

How We Start vs. How We Continue

It is important to note here that how we start does not necessarily dictate how we will finish. For example, you can be one of those people who needs to focus singly on one task or project until you get a really good handle on it and then once you have that under way, you may feel that now you can take on something else as well.

The main thing is to be working diligently on that thing or those things, and to not cut corners. When we cut corners, it becomes very obvious and the result(s) will definitely be lackluster. When we do something in a lackluster kind of way, the final product shows that there was a lack of work, planning and execution involved, and that does not work well for anyone.

If you notice that things are not going the best with taking on more, there is nothing wrong with switching gears and acknowledging from as early on as possible that this is not working and that we need to go back to focusing on only the one thing. It is far better to do that than to continue with something that isn't making sense and that isn't working. Being an overachiever and getting it done does not have to mean we do many projects at once - it simply means that we do what we need to in an effort to get things done and done well.

Chapter 20

Discover What And/Or Who Inspires You

Being inspired by something or someone is a gift. Being inspired by something or someone is one thing that will propel us to do greater things in our own lives. Whether it's a person or a thing that helps us realize our passion, helps us see how we want to do something or we see how a person demonstrates their own passion for something, being inspired is a gift and it's wonderful.

Inspiration can come from anywhere. We can meet a person for a moment and have a lifetime of being inspired by them. Finding your inspiration is such a great gift and while the person or thing helps to open us up, it does not necessarily mean that we have to do things in the exact same way as them. I found inspiration in Joel Osteen and Joyce Meyer and I love to preach the application of the Gospel in every facet of life but it does not mean that my method will be exactly the same as either of them.

Who are the people who inspire you? Is it a person or persons? Is it a pet? Is it someone you knew long ago or someone you met recently? The person who inspires you may be a controversial person (I remember when I went to a Starbucks location to sit and read with a book in my hand written by Donald Trump and the cashier literally suggested I may not want to be seen in the location with that book in my hand). A person can make such a comment but it is not necessary for you to accept it and comply with what they may be suggesting.

Another thing to think about is why does that person inspire you? You may discover from researching a bit about a person that their words and their actions are not quite as inspiring as you thought they would be. I remember following some people on social media because they possessed characteristics I found to be appealing but in the end, when I took a closer look at some of their choices, I found that they were not the person for me. So, when you look at a person that inspires you, it will tell you a lot about yourself. It will tell a lot about the values you hold dear.

A friend of mine I will name Alma found two politicians to be fascinating and she said that they inspired her with many of their ideas. I encouraged her to look a little more into both of their values and his platforms, not just who they appear to be on the surface. She did that and found that many of the ideas presented by one were totally out of whack with her own value system and she did not feel as drawn to them anymore. Subsequently, upon visiting the profile pages and researching the other politician, she found that this one's platform was much more in line with her values and she even began working for one of them on their campaign. Know who you are supporting and whose values are closely tied to your own. A person's values and principles do matter and do make a difference in every part of what they do.

Biblical Inspiration

If you do not already know Jesus, I encourage you to read the Bible and to consider whether He might serve as your inspiration. Also, look carefully at the character profiles of those mentioned in the Bible and see if one or more of them may serve as your inspiration. One of the amazing things about the disciples that Jesus chose were ordinary people. Jesus chose ordinary people with ordinary jobs to follow Him and to be part of His entourage. When you carefully consider that these ordinary people have really done some extraordinary things, we can feel quite inspired by them and we can use this as our source of inspiration.

Consider Mary. This was an ordinary woman through whom God decided to bring forth His chosen One, His Son who would save the world. A perfectly ordinary woman.

Consider Abraham. This was an ordinary man who had faults and made mistakes like you and I and look carefully on how God brought miracles out of his story.

Consider David. An ordinary shepherd boy overlooked by his own family and how God brought something so amazing from him.

I encourage you to read through the Bible (free copies are available to those who ask for it and can be sent to you via mail or you can download a Bible app on your smartphone) - I use the brown icon Holy Bible app and keep that on my smartphone. Seeing as the Bible is the wisest book ever created, reading it more than one is highly recommended. Each time you read it, you will likely take different things from it, and you will be opening yourself up to new learning that the Holy Spirit brings to your attention.

How do you make sure the Holy Spirit brings these things to your attention? Pray for it to be so. Here is a suggested prayer: *"God, I am trying to get to know You. I would like to read the Holy Bible and would like to ask You to let the Holy Spirit speak to me clearly about anything You want to bring to my attention and any take-aways you want me to pull from my readings. I thank You in advance for the revelations and insights You will bring to me. In Jesus' name. Amen"*

Write Them Down

A last word about what inspires you: write down the names of those who inspire you. Write them down so that you can remember them and so that you have a record of them. It is possible that these change over time but knowing this information now is a tell on where you are today and how you may change in future.

Chapter 21

Glory To God

We must always give glory to God. In all cases and in all situations, we need to give the glory to God because He is the One who brought us these goals, He is the One who is helping us and guiding us to accomplish all these things and He is the One who is ultimately making it happen.

God never gives us a dream or a goal that fits neatly within the resources we have at our immediate disposal. He will always give you dreams that are much bigger, much grander than what you currently have the resources for. As such, He is ultimately the One who is going to make those dreams happen for you and for the betterment of society. See, God knows that people are watching, waiting, listening and expecting. He knows that they are looking and waiting to see how He plays out in your life. Your testimony of how He works in your life is very important and God knows others are waiting for your testimony so that they too can see that they need to rely on Him. Knowing this, when He does show up in our lives, we must give Him the glory. We must really be clear and show that we are giving Him the glory. It is our way of honoring Him.

It is our way of acknowledging His work in our lives and our faith in Him.

A Note About Testimonials

Not only is it important to provide your testimonial, it is also really important to provide the details. What I mean by this is that it is important to include all the details about the situation so that people can see all the challenges, difficulties and trials you went through and how God helped you through all of them.

Acknowledging His involvement does not take anything away from your abilities as a doer and an overachiever. Not in the least. In fact, it also honors and elevates you because you are another ordinary person through whom God did extraordinary things.

So I encourage you to provide your testimonial when you are on the other side of those challenges. Write down specific details (as much as you are comfortable providing), timelines, guidance you feel you received from the Holy Spirit and any other details you feel you need to provide.

At the end of the day, the glory is HIS!

Chapter 22

Going Back

Sometimes in life, we miss our calling. There may have been unfortunate situations, there may have been inopportune timing so we may have missed a piece (or all of) our calling.

What to do? What do we do if we have made a mistake and we realize that we have missed our calling or we realize that we did not see something through to completion that needed to be completed?

Simple. You go back.

One of the wonderful things about life and life in partnership with God is that we can go back and fix something that you realize needs fixing.

We can go back and complete that degree or that certificate.
We can go back and make amends when & where it needs to be made.
We can go back and start or revive that dream of having your own business.

We can go back and work on having that baby or that child you dreamed of.

We can go back and work on righting a wrong that was made, on a road missed, and more.

As long as your will is there to fix something or to do something about it and God is saying the way is still open, there is a way. If God says that that way is not still open, He will either open it or give you another. He is not a God who will just slam the door in your face and say "Too bad!"

Many people go through life thinking that because they experienced a failure or because they experienced a setback, that that's it, their time is up, there is no going back. That is wrong thinking. Think with hope. Think with expectation. Remember that most things (if not all things) can be fixed, can be rectified. Wrongs can be made right.

Forgiveness

One area that I know plagues many people is the area of forgiveness, or rather, unforgiveness. People wrongly think that by forgiving someone, that we have allowed them to get away with what they have done.

Not so.

Forgiving simply means that we are not going to let it hurt us anymore. A wise thing to do would be to reflect on it, forgive the person or the situation and then let God deal with them. God can change that person's life, can cause them to realize their errors, and can restore all that needs to be restored in a way that you cannot. I'm not saying that God is going to hurt them or destroy them. I am saying that God is Sovereign and He knows how to right a wrong, and on top of it, He controls everything so He is the perfect One who can help in this case.

If something is on your mind like that, why not say *"God, I am giving this problem to you. I am giving you the hurt, the pain, the failure, the bad feelings....I am giving it all to You."*

God does not call us to right wrongs in our own strength but instead, to trust Him to do that for us. He sees that wrong and He knew it would be coming long before it happened. It was not a surprise to Him.

He knew you would make mistakes long before you ever made them and He made a provision for that. It's called relying on Jesus. So if you think you have missed something, you made a mistake, you want to right a wrong, it is not too late. Even if the person is not here with us anymore, you can still right it by writing a letter, praying, visiting the person's grave and much more.

Picking Up Where You Left Off

When we have realized that we made a mistake or that we missed an opportunity, we can go back and fix it by looking into where things stand.
Put that business idea to the side and thought it was dead? Check in on it and see where things stand and how you and God together can revive it.

Let someone special go that God keeps putting on your heart? Check in on it and see where things stand and how you and God together can revive it.

Always wanted to have that baby but thought the doctor's report was final? Check in on it and see where things stand and how you and God together can revive it.

Wanted to finish that degree or certificate but left it halfway through? Check in on it and see where things stand and how you and God together can revive it.

Made a mistake and treated someone unfairly that didn't deserve it? Check in on it and see where things stand and how you and God together can revive it.

Realized you were unfair to your spouse and now you feel you need to fix it? Check in on it and see where things stand so you can see how you and God together can revive it.

Said something inappropriate to someone in the heat of the moment? Check in on it and see where things stand and how you and God together can fix it.

As you can see, there is always a way to fix any situation. So do not sit there being upset about it, worried about it, letting it fester. Talk to God about it and move forward in the way or ways He tells you to.

Images

Some images to help you - feel free to print these out, post them around your living space and use them as you feel you need to to keep yourself motivated. Remember that we are all visual creators and images help us contextualize everything and help the concept be more ingrained in our thoughts and our minds.

organize and decorate everything

Vision Board

For I know the plans I have for you, declares the Lord, plans to *prosper* you not to harm you, plans to give you *hope* and a *future*

Jeremiah 29:11

GOD'S GOT MY BACK

I believe that God will do the impossible in my life.

Write Amen if you believe!

YOUR
ONLY
LIMIT
IS YOU

DON'T TELL PEOPLE YOUR DREAMS. SHOW THEM.

surround yourself with people who believe in your dreams

IG|MotivationWall

Jesus
is my *joy*, my *life*, my *peace* and my EVERYTHING

Whenever i am afraid, i **trust** in *You.*

Psalm 56:3

HAVE THE COURAGE TO BEGIN AGAIN

Notes

This section is entirely dedicated to your notes. Reflect, write out your thoughts, motivations, Scriptures, etc. Scribble, write in print, write in cursive, do as you will...it is your space to write out things that come to you as you read, post-reading, or just musings you have about the content and how it relates to your life.

Notes ~ 163

Thanks

Thanks for taking the time to read my book. I hope it has helped you and that you put its concepts into practice. I pray that the concepts, explanations, Scriptures used and more work well in helping you understand and that the Holy Spirit speaks to you clearly and always.

Dr. Christine Topjian

www.ingramcontent.com/pod-product-compliance
Lightning Source LLC
Chambersburg PA
CBHW050418120526
44590CB00015B/2018